Date: _____

Dear _____,

By the time you reach the age I am now, you may notice some disturbing changes in your life. While every life stage has its adjustments, this one can be a bit more challenging. This one, most likely, is menopause. It can be surprising, confusing, and frustrating.

When you experience this, I hope to talk with you, to answer your questions, to give you practical advice for this vexing adjustment. I do know, however, that some of my experiences, upon remembrance, may seem fuzzy or faraway. So I've written them down for you.

I give you Postcards from Menopause. They include notes from my experiences, and they will help you understand my journey through menopause. I hope you find them helpful as you make decisions, talk with your doctors, and consider your genetic heritage.

So, read and enjoy. Ask me anything.

With love and prayers,

Postcards from MENOPAUSE
Wishing I Weren't Here

Lois Mowday Rabey

FAMILYLIFE™
Publishing

Little Rock, Arkansas

2003 Published by FamilyLife, a division of Campus Crusade for Christ.

ISBN: 1-57229-501-5

Author: Lois Mowday Rabey
Editor: Amy Bradford
Editorial Assistants: Fran Taylor, Robyn Stutts
Proofreaders: Fran Taylor, Sharon Hill, Susan Matthews
Cover Design and Interior Layout: Jerome L. Nelson
Design Assistant: Jerry McCall
Photography: Dan Butkowski
Additional Photography: Courtesy of Getty Images

Printed in the United States of America.

11 10   09   08   07   06   05   04   03   5   4   3   2   1

FAMILYLIFE™
Publishing

Dennis Rainey, President
5800 Ranch Dr.
Little Rock, AR 72223
1-800-FL-TODAY
www.familylife.com
A division of Campus Crusade for Christ

This book is dedicated to

Ann Reed

She aged so gracefully that
those of us who knew her
were not even aware that she
was getting any older.

Contents

Preface vii

Acknowledgments ix

Introduction xi

1. What Is Happening to Me? 1

2. Hot and Cold and All Shook Up 21

3. Mind, Waist, and Emotions—What Next? 39

4. Startling Medical News 59

5. The Process for Making Informed Decisions 71

6. Treatment Options 91

7. Preventative Measures: Diet and Exercise 109

8. Relaxation Breaks: By Yourself, with Others,
   with God 119

9. I Don't Want to Talk
   to Men About Menopause 137

10. What Wives Wish Their Husbands Knew and a
    Mindset Metamorphosis for Every Grown-Up . . .147

11. Some Things Husbands Wish They Knew
    by Steve Rabey 161

12. Looking for Relief and Power 179

13. Facing Mortality 197

14. Women Take a Look Back 207

Appendix A: Starting a Support Group 215

Appendix B: Using Postcards from Menopause 217

Notes 219

PREFACE

This book was first published under the title *Coming of Age,* and I wrote it when I was smack in the middle of menopause. Symptoms abounded and emotions wailed. I found that many other women were also grasping to understand what was going on in their bodies, minds, and spirits just as I was. And so this book was born.

Since then, issues that I raised in the first edition have become front-page news stories. Medical opinions on treatment have changed radically, and women are concerned. They speak more openly now than they did a decade ago, and they want help and answers.

With each breaking news story on menopause and treatment, it is becoming increasingly evident that each woman needs to become her own best advocate. In doing that, she needs help in making informed choices.

Because of these new and confusing medical findings, and because a new decade of women faces menopause, I decided to revise this book. It is now released under the title *Postcards from Menopause: Wishing I Weren't Here.*

The original introduction is basically the same, even though I am a number of years down the road from that frightening day in a Denver bookstore. The rest of the book contains updated material.

I hope you will laugh, cry, reflect, and make personal choices about your own health as you read my journey through menopause. You are not alone and help is available.

ACKNOWLEDGMENTS

I especially want to thank the wonderful people at FamilyLife who asked me to write an updated version of this book. I appreciate their interest and concern about this topic and their desire to provide support for women during this particular life passage.

It has been a delight to work with Amy Bradford, a woman much too young to need this information herself, but one who expressed enthusiasm from our first conversation. Thank you, Amy, for your sweet spirit as well as professionalism ... not always an easy mix, but you do it beautifully.

A big thank you to the women I interviewed this time around. You know who you are, and I thank you for your willingness to look back at a former time in your lives.

In a book like this, professional opinion is always needed, and I especially thank Dr. Lisa Dunham, Dr. Bruce Kahn, and Chris Strong. A special "thank you" goes to Erika Van Hulzen who persevered in connecting me with Dr. Kahn.

And, of course, my family ... Steve, Chadd and Lisa, Lara and Craig, and the seven shining stars in our family galaxy: Justin, Alex, Brady, and Dylan Miller; and Lisa, Nathan, and Cole Van Hulzen. Your loving support in all areas of my life continues to bring many smiles, even when I'm in the middle of a project.

INTRODUCTION

This was written as I first embarked on my menopause journey.

I Need THAT Book!

I am neither shy nor easily embarrassed. In fact, sometimes I cause others to blush because of my feisty relational style. People never need wonder what I'm thinking because I will tell them if they hang around me longer than thirty seconds.

But, a few months ago I found myself in an unusual situation. My husband, Steve, and I went to visit The Tattered Cover, a bookstore in Denver. It is a four-story paradise of volume-filled shelves, over-stuffed chairs, dark wood accouterments, and an eclectic clientele.

As we approached the front door, I stopped and pulled Steve out of the way of the stream of ingoing customers.

"I want you to get a book for me," I said in a low tone. He looked a little puzzled.

"I don't want to ask for it myself, and I don't want to go up and pay for it myself."

Steve scrunched his eyebrows together until lines in his forehead appeared.

"Why?" he finally managed to ask.

"I don't want anyone to know," I said, glancing over my shoulder like a character in a French spy novel.

"Lois, what are you talking about?"

"I want Gail Sheehy's book, *Silent Passage,* about—you know—uh—women my age. Actually, it's about women a little older than I am—you know—50 or so—but I am almost there and I feel—you know."

"No, I don't know," he said, "and, I think it's okay for you to ask for it yourself."

Terror! He wasn't going to cooperate. He slipped from my grasp, moved through the revolving doors, and disappeared into the store before I could plead my case.

"Steve!" I called as I ran to catch up with him, "Wait, you have to help me. Just get the book for me and that will be the end of it."

"The end of what?" he asked with the same puzzled look on his face.

He doesn't know, I thought. *I haven't really told him that I am embarrassed to be old enough to need to read a book about women "that age."*

"Oh, never mind," I said out loud.

Steve looked relieved. We decided to meet by the first floor check-out desk in an hour. I was surprised—I had to have that book, but I was actually sweating over the prospect of someone seeing me buy it. There was some painful kind of recognition taking place—I was admitting to the world what the world already knew: Women face significant and sometimes distressing changes between the ages of forty and fifty-five due to the process of menopause; and I (youthful, active, energetic) had reached that stage where I was going through some of those changes.

I had been thinking that if I didn't admit to the discomfort I was experiencing, no one would think that I was aging. How silly! The evidence was there: my hair was white; my children were grown; I was about to become a grandmother; my skin showed the unmistakable signs of weathering.

The only one I was kidding was myself. Admitting that I wanted some advice on this subject did not reveal any revolutionary secret to anyone but me. I was shocked at my own resistance to the inevitable. My life had included several dramatic changes that I always handled with a degree of calm. Now, here I was in the middle of a crowded bookstore, sweating and feeling nervous over buying a book.

My desire for the book motivated me up the stairs to the second floor. But in a store that carries over 225,000 titles, finding the general topic would be challenge enough. I knew that I wanted the area devoted to women's studies, but I couldn't find it. Panic surfaced again as I realized that I would have to ask for help.

How old am I? I scolded myself, feeling insecure and thirteen.

I finally found a workstation with two female salesclerks at the computer terminals. I didn't want a man even to hear me ask for the book. I quietly asked one of the women if they had the book *Silent Passage.* She immediately headed across the room with me in tow like a bashful child.

The women's section covered seven long shelves. I quickly picked up *Silent Passage* and moved away from the telltale area. As I continued to browse through the bookstore, I kept my arm tightly wrapped around the book so no one could see the title. An hour later, Steve and I met at the checkout counter, and I handed him the book. He took it without question and put it with his stack of purchases. I lingered around the fiction section until he was done. We left, and my discomfort ended. Temporarily.

Breaking the Silence

Only a few weeks later, I began to have some symptoms that were mentioned in Sheehy's book: anxiety, memory loss, mood swings. And just like the title says, I remained silent. But the isolation made me feel crazy. Why did I not hear other women talk about feeling these things? I knew I couldn't be the only one in my circle of friends who felt this way. So, I broke the silence and began to ask other women my age if they were experiencing any of these strange new interruptions to normalcy.

"Yes, yes!" one after another excitedly replied, relieved that they, too, were not alone.

Venturing into conversations with these women led to the writing of this book. I interviewed over 100 women and heard at least that many variations of the way they handled moving through the mid-life years. These women talked about menopause and its impact on all areas of their lives—thinking, decisions, relationships.

I also talked with some men about their feelings as their wives faced menopause.

The stories of these men and women, and my own, are woven through this book. (The names have been changed, but the stories are written as they were told.) Some of them are funny, some tragic, each showing how unique and personal menopause is.

Perhaps you are thinking, *Menopause? What's the big deal? I'll simply proceed the way I always have.*

That was my attitude. I had never thought seriously about menopause because I didn't know that much about it. I knew that I didn't intend to grow old the way I had seen some women do. I told myself for years that I simply would not gain weight, would not become an emotional basket case, and would not be fazed by the life changes that would occur. My faith in God's provision and my moxie would carry me through.

Then one day, as I dissolved one-time-too-many in a puddle of tears, I had to admit that my old ways of coping were not enough to get me through this new, unique experience. Something was missing. I began to question my ability to appropriate my faith. I flogged myself for falling short of peaceful calm and failing to rise above my circumstances. I had always been able to draw on spiritual truth and God's promises to overcome anything, including the death of my first husband.

But, now, I felt disconnected from God when something as simple as an emotional low occurred. I prayed and paced and panicked, and finally I realized that I needed information, encouragement, and help.

God was there in the panic. He is here now, and He will be with me always. Many of the women I interviewed experienced the same spiritual self-doubt as they stumbled through these years of disruption. Their stories, and mine, are testimonies to the steadfastness of God. He accepts us in our frustration, our doubt, our learning, and our changes. As in all things, He uses it to our good.

I still cannot believe I am in my late forties. It seems like my recent 30-year high school reunion should have been my 10-year reunion. I watch football games and feel like the cheerleader I once was so long ago. I hold a baby, and I picture my own children (who are now in their twenties) as infants. I visit my dad in his nursing home and I'm shocked that I am the parent figure, and he is like a child.

I accept where I am in this new life-phase. I try to think and act like a mature woman. But sometimes—inside, unseen, unheard—I scream to myself, *I'm too young to be this old!*

These were my earliest symptoms, how I noticed them, and when they began …

Date: _____

Hello from Springfield, Ohio!
It's my first chance to meet Steve's hometown
buddies, and where am I? The ladies room.
Every 10 minutes. Oh, to be in the comfort
of home.
Wishing I weren't here—

Lois

CHAPTER 1

What Is Happening to Me?

Technically speaking, menopause is the cessation of a woman's menstrual cycle, occurring sometime between the ages of 40 and 55. But the internal changes that culminate in this event begin many years earlier. These internal changes can produce symptoms that appear one month and may not return until many months later. The woman may be alarmed by the symptoms and surprised to find out they are related to menopause.

That's what happened to me.

Surprised and Afraid

I was 43 years old, a bride again of four months, and feeling great. I was looking forward to visiting my husband's hometown in Ohio. It was a combination work and pleasure trip, as I was speaking on Sunday morning in the church where he had accepted Christ years ago.

We arrived on a Friday, a beautiful fall afternoon. The trees had just begun to change colors, and the air held a slight chill. We enjoyed a few hours of nostalgic remembrances for Steve as we visited his childhood homes, his high school, his college, and his favorite haunts. That night we joined his family for a leisurely dinner at their favorite restaurant. All indications were that we had a relaxing weekend ahead of us.

In the middle of the night, I woke up feeling bloated and slightly uncomfortable. I went to the bathroom and was surprised to find that I was bleeding heavily. My period, always uneventful and easy, should have lightened and ended soon. By morning, I had been up a few more times and continued to be perplexed by the heavy bleeding. Otherwise, I felt fine; no cramps, no other symptoms at all.

We began our day of scheduled visits to a number of Steve's friends. I assumed I would be fine, so long as I made a restroom stop every hour or so. But by three o'clock that afternoon, I couldn't make it more than ten minutes. I was alarmed and embarrassed that, in front of strangers, I had to excuse myself to go to the bathroom continually. Finally, I told Steve that I was a little scared and thought I should go to a 24-hour emergency medical office. There was no way I could speak the next day if the bleeding continued at the same rate.

On the way to the clinic, I was afraid and confused. I had never had any trouble whatsoever with my period. All I knew about abnormal bleeding was that it could indicate cancer. I envisioned a huge tumor in my body about to explode. I had no physical pain, but emotionally, I was in agony.

We arrived at the clinic, and I felt a measure of relief in knowing help was at hand. As soon as I had filled out the registration information, the receptionist put me in a room to see the doctor. I was embarrassed at the thought of being examined by a stranger when I was such a mess. The nurse was very sympathetic. "Don't worry, the doctor sees a number of women for similar emergencies."

Similar to what? I asked myself. I had never heard any woman say anything about this kind of episode.

The doctor was pleasant and reassuring. He said the heavy bleeding was probably a hormonal imbalance related to my age. I remember thinking to myself, *My age? What about my age?* I didn't ask him what he meant. I just wanted him to fix my problem.

He gave me a hormone shot and told me to see my own doctor as soon as I got home. I promised him that I would. I also persisted in getting him to promise me that I would not be embarrassed as I stood in front of a church full of people the next morning. He promised.

"You'll dry up like a desert in an hour or so," he said.

I was exhausted. Steve and I canceled our evening plans and went back to our hotel. We ate in the room and watched television. I was preoccupied with worry about making it through the next day's speaking engagement and the plane ride home.

Fortunately the doctor was right. My body reacted to the shot in the manner of a gushing faucet having been turned off suddenly. The bleeding stopped completely. It wasn't until we were on the plane on the way home that I wondered again about the cause. *It couldn't be related to menopause, because that only had to do with hot flashes and the cessation of bleeding. Besides, menopause happened to older women, not to me at the age of 43.* I was worried that the bleeding was a sign of cancer.

I called my doctor first thing Monday morning. Tuesday morning I was in her office telling her of my harrowing experience. Since the bleeding had been so heavy, she suggested one of two things: a biopsy to rule out cancer or a D and C (dilatation and curettage—scraping of the uterus) to not only rule out cancer, but to help prevent future bleeding episodes. I tend to make quick decisions and remained in character that day.

"Let's go for the D and C and get this over with," I said assertively, confident that my temporary problem would be over. My doctor thought I would be fine to have the procedure done in her office with local anesthesia.

My husband and I arrived at the doctor's office on the appointed morning. By that time, I had grown nervous about the procedure. The day before, I had talked with a friend who had had a D and C. She swore she would never again have one without general anesthesia. She wanted to be completely knocked out. I decided to keep my appointment and persevere with my plans, but her words lingered in my mind.

I was given a shot to calm me and make me feel sleepy. It worked; I was barely awake. The procedure was uncomfortable, but not painful. Time blurred completely. When it was over, I had to be led to the car by my husband. I immediately fell asleep on the ride home.

The D and C revealed no evidence of cancer. The diagnosis was "hormonal changes." It may be hard to believe that I didn't ask any questions. But at that time, I accepted it to mean my hormones were fluctuating and no other symptoms would occur. Just in case another incident did occur, however, my doctor prescribed birth control pills, which contain hormones, to have on hand. Taking one or two of them would stop any unexpected bleeding.*

Life went back to normal, and I almost forgot the whole incident. The bleeding, which I now know was hemorrhaging, happened again about a year later. This time I had the birth control pills with me. Once again, I was out of town for a speaking engagement, so when I returned home, I called my doctor. This time she did a biopsy instead of a D and C. (A biopsy examines the

---

*Always consult with your doctor thoroughly. If there is a possibility that you are pregnant when bleeding occurs, taking medications with hormones is dangerous.

tissue to rule out cancer. It does nothing to prevent further bleeding.) Again, thankfully, no cancer. The diagnosis: hormonal.

Unlike my experience with the D and C, the biopsy actually caused more bleeding. This, too, is normal, but it was nonetheless disconcerting. I became apprehensive about future episodes of unexpected hemorrhaging and carried tampons with me all the time, along with the magic pills that would shut off the spigot. There were three more incidents in four years, and all three occurred when I was traveling. I learned that this is a normal, early symptom of menopause.

In the years following that first sign, I lived with a general sense of watchfulness. Other symptoms kicked in, including anxiety attacks, dizziness, and forgetfulness. There was no pattern or consistency with any of these interruptions. Anytime, anywhere, I could start bleeding, sweating, feeling dizzy, or emoting dramatically.

Nothing is permanent but change.
—Heraclitus

This probably doesn't sound like good news. But by being informed and preparing for what is to come, much of the fear and uncertainty of the beginning phases of menopause can be alleviated.

The Beginning of a Process

The first symptoms of menopause signal the beginning of a process that can last for several years.

In the book *Managing Your Menopause,* Dr. Wulf Utian and Ruth S. Jacobowitz define the word that is used to describe this entire process.

> The word "climacteric" comes from the Greek and means "critical time." Sometime during this so-called critical time (generally a ten-year span between the ages of forty-five and fifty-five) your last period will occur—usually when you're around the age of 50. But changes are happening long before that time, and beginning in your thirties, you may not only notice them but you can do something about them.[1]

The process unfolds this way:

1. Sometime during the age range of the thirties, forties, or fifties, a woman's body begins to produce less estrogen than it has since the onset of menstruation.

2. The levels of estrogen production can fluctuate over a period of years, called the *climacteric.*

3. These fluctuating levels of estrogen result in changes that manifest themselves in numerous symptoms.

4. Eventually the body stops producing estrogen completely and menstruation occurs for the last time. This event is called *menopause.*

Often the word *menopause* is used to refer to the entire process of the climacteric. That is how the process is defined in this book.

Understanding menopause and how to respond to it can help a woman move through the process more smoothly than a woman who begins with little warning or knowledge. But why don't women know more about this process?

Our Heritage of Silence

My mother was from the old school. You know, the one that touted the doctrine: *You should never talk about religion, politics, or sex.* I never questioned her. I accepted that these subjects were off-limits. While religion and politics filtered into our dinner-time conversations occasionally, s-e-x *never* did.

My parents' involvement in my sex education consisted of my mother slipping me a book when I was 12 and telling me to read it. I remember it being excessively technical and boring, with no pictures or sketches, which was disappointing. Of course, the other kids at school had long ago told me about the "birds and the bees." So, after a week, I handed it back to my mother without a word. She took it, and that was that.

When I was growing up, my mother never mentioned menopause. It might be assumed that as one's own mother entered this life passage, a daughter would hear (or overhear) what was happening. I did not. My mother was rushed to the hospital one morning when I was 10 years old. She was 46 and had some sudden, secret something happen in the middle of the night. My father took her to the hospital, and I stayed home with my grandmother, who helped keep the secret. When my father came home later that day, he told me she had undergone a hysterectomy and would be home soon. I didn't know what a hysterectomy was, nor did I ask. I was simply glad when she came home and all was well again.

Both my mother and father treated any sexual subjects as shameful. The fact that menopause involves a woman's sex organs would have been enough to keep them silent.

Many women now over the age of forty or fifty grew up in households similar to mine. I know because I interviewed over 100 of them for this book. Their parents did not talk about sex, and their mothers did not talk about their menopause when it occurred. Some of these women have since asked their mothers about this taboo topic. The ones whose mothers talked freely after the fact described symptoms like those their daughters experienced. The main difference was that those women suffered in silence.

Using Postcards from Menopause

Now we live in a different time, where s-e-x and m-e-n-o-p-a-u-s-e are discussed a little more openly. Well, sex is, anyway—menopause, less so. To help you bridge this conversation with your daughter, I've included a set of Postcards from Menopause in this book. To use them, answer the questions or journal about the suggested topics on each card, then send the cards to your daughter or a younger woman who has yet to experience these changes. (If you need more sets of cards for daughters two and three, call 1-800-FL-TODAY or log on to www.familylife.com.)

If you're approaching menopause, it may be that your daughter is busy chasing toddlers; she may not feel that an in-depth discussion on menopause is relevant right now. If she doesn't seem interested, suggest that she tuck these cards away. In ten or twenty years she'll wonder, *What did Mom go through? Is this normal?* At that time, she'll be grateful for your in-the-moment writings on your experiences. Hopefully, you'll be there to answer any questions she may have, but if you're not, she'll appreciate your forethought in preparing her for this life stage. She'll be relieved to know that you did not suffer in silence, and neither should she.

Menopausal women were described as hysterical females who were over-sexed, self-indulgent, and subject to madness.

To better understand why our mothers and grandmothers endured this change without a word, let's look at the way menopausal women were portrayed in recent history.

Recent History's Portrayal of the Menopausal Woman

At the beginning of the twentieth century, many people (men *and* women) thought that menopause equaled insanity. Menopausal women were described as hysterical females who were over-sexed, self-indulgent, and subject to madness.

One of the popular books of the day, *The Dangerous Age,* a novel by Karin Michaelis, was published in 1911. The central character, Elsie Lindtner, divorces her husband and runs away with a younger man. This behavior is attributed to her mad state as a result of her age.

Lois Banner describes Elsie and her friends in Banner's book, *In Full Flower.*

> As the novel progresses, most of Lindtner's middle-aged women friends suffer emotional breakdowns. Some alternate between mania and depression; some leave their husbands. Some become obsessive; one woman cleans her house over and over again. Another is institutionalized and treated surgically.[2]

This view was so prevalent in the early 1900s that it was reflected in the name chosen for the surgery common to women between the ages of 40 and 50—*hysterectomy.* Lois Banner explains how this word came into existence.

> Michaelis's presentation of menopause as producing insanity resonated in the views of many gynecologists. Drawing on misperceptions standard for centuries, many gynecologists posited a direct linkage between the uterus and the brain. (Such a belief would result in the term "hysterectomy" for the removal of the uterus and ovaries, referencing the mental condition of hysteria and its presumed connection to female reproductive organs.) And such beliefs were extended to aging women.[3]

Not everyone agreed with this negative picture of menopausal women. In 1912, the opposite image was popularized in the book *Woman's Share in Social Culture* by Anna Garlin Spencer. Lois Banner describes this view:

"Spencer drew from contemporary evidence that women lived longer than men and were more vital in older years to assert that menopause afforded women a 'second youth.'"[4]

These conflicting views of menopausal women continued to cause confusion. Banner continues, "The first opinion has been that menopause is an illness bringing a breakdown of body and mind. The second has been that menopause initiates a time of strength for women ... "[5]

By the 1930s and 1940s, it seemed that the first opinion was winning the popularity poll. Growing numbers of women were being diagnosed as insane due to menopause. Hospitals had whole sections for mentally disturbed, menopausal women.

I can understand why my mother and other women her age decided to keep quiet about any menopausal symptoms they were experiencing. They could have found themselves institutionalized as a result of speaking out.

What Does the Bible Say?

Menopause is not mentioned directly in the Bible, but there are two examples of women who bore children after they were no longer of childbearing age: Sarah in the Old Testament and Elizabeth in the New Testament.

In the Old Testament we read, "Now Abraham and Sarah were old, well advanced in age; and Sarah had passed the age of childbearing" (Genesis 18:11). God intervened, and Sarah gave birth to Isaac.

In the New Testament, Elizabeth is also past childbearing age. Her husband, Zacharias, is visited by an angel who tells him that he and Elizabeth will have a son. Zacharias replies, "How shall I know this? For I am an old man, and my wife is well advanced in years" (Luke 1:18).

These passages are silent with regard to menopause except to show that God chose to intervene in the lives of both these women and give them children even after they were old. But, while the Bible is silent about menopause, it has much to say about age.

When my daughter, Lara, was in the sixth grade, she had to find a Bible verse that described her mother. At the end of the school day, she proudly brought her paper home to me with her verse describing me. "The silver-haired head is a crown of glory, if it is found in the way of righteousness" (Proverbs 16:31).

> *Every age has its pleasures, its style of wit, and its own ways.*
> —*Nicolas Boileau*

I was 38 years old at the time, but my hair was very gray. (I have always preferred to call it white.) Lara beamed up at me as I read her paper. I smiled, hugged her, and thanked her for thinking of me as righteous, evidenced, in part, by my silver crown.

It was a mixed blessing: My daughter admired me but described me as aged. The incident made me realize that the Bible does have some positive things to say about aging. Older people are presented as possessing wisdom worthy of respect:

> Wisdom is with aged men, and with length
> of days, understanding. —Job 12:12

> You shall rise before the gray headed and
> honor the presence of an old man, and fear
> your God: I am the Lord. —Leviticus 19:32

But, it also acknowledges declining health in old age.

> Now the eyes of Israel were dim with age,
> so that he could not see. —Genesis 48:10

> Do not cast me off in the time of old age;
> do not forsake me when my strength fails.
> —Psalm 71:9

Perhaps the most well-known biblical text that describes a godly woman is Proverbs 31. This passage focuses on the character of a wise woman, not her physical condition. It lifts up the qualities of virtue, industriousness, wisdom, kindness, and fear of the Lord.

The Bible paints a picture that defines women without reference to menopause and uplifts both men and women who attain an old age. But current society has not pursued the same ideals.

A Culture Obsessed with Youth

America worships the cult of youth. The cosmetic industry is a prime example of turning that worship into a money-making endeavor. One of the target markets for cosmetic companies is the menopausal woman. There are anti-aging products for every body part, with advertisements claiming miraculous results from the daily use of these gold-priced wonder creams.

A few years ago I ordered a body lotion from a store in Florida because this particular product line is not sold in my home state of Colorado. When the package arrived in the mail, it contained fourteen additional samples of different anti-aging potions.

There were creams for the eyes, nose, mouth, elbows, hands, feet, thighs, legs, and "special" creams to boot. Evidently each cream knew how to work on its designated body part—but not on any other. Heaven forbid that you mix up your eye cream with your thigh cream. No telling what would happen.

I sadly confess that I have tried a number of these panaceas for aging. I have now faced the stark reality that, of course, they don't work. Why have I wasted money on such foolishness? Because I have bought into the American dream that says youth is the only form of acceptable beauty. I swallowed the cosmetic companies' claims of regaining a youthful appearance with their wonder creams.

Intellectually and spiritually I know that this is not true, but it is difficult to dash the hope of looking forever young.

Attitudes Are Changing

Fortunately, I am changing my mind, and I am beginning to give up my quest for the fountain of youth in a bottle. While writing this book, I met the most engaging women who unashamedly accept the physical results of aging, and they do it with style. They don't

15

> *I met the most engaging women who unashamedly accept the physical results of aging, and they do it with style.*

worry about wrinkles or a little weight gain. They take care of themselves physically but operate on the truth that beauty *is* more than skin deep. Advertising may be targeting older women with the promise of looking younger, but many older women are focusing on far more fulfilling arenas. They are trying to improve in areas of life where they can learn and grow instead of trying to be something they are not.

For many menopausal women, aging and beauty began to take a back seat in July of 2002 when the medical community announced that using hormone replacement therapy (HRT) increased their risk of breast cancer, heart attack, stroke, and blood clots.[6] With that discovery, treating menopausal symptoms *safely* became far more important than minimizing laugh lines or crows' feet.

On a list of priorities, effective and safe treatment for menopause certainly outranks disguising age. And that, I've found, is just not possible, as my next story tells.

Senior Discount!

Early on in my menopause journey, I had been visiting my daughters in San Diego and was driving on to Palm Springs. The drive wasn't taking as long as I anticipated, so along the way I stopped at an outlet mall to browse through the stores. I felt good and was particularly proud of myself for exercising that morning—I was sticking to my exercise routine, even away from home.

Date: _____

RECEIVE

These were my feelings and emotions as I entered this season …

One jewelry store displayed enticing signs that announced discounts of 40 percent to 60 percent off each purchase. I picked out some earrings for my daughters and myself and went up to the counter. The clerk, a woman about my age at the time, smiled and rang up my items with the discounts. Then she said brightly, "And, you get an additional 10 percent off!"

"Oh, great!" I smiled back. "How come?"

She turned and pointed to a little sign on the wall behind her.

TUESDAY IS SENIOR DISCOUNT DAY
ADDITIONAL 10% OFF

I was shocked. My heart started to race, and I had to stifle the urge to punch this friendly lady right in the mouth. *Senior Discount! Is she kidding? I wasn't even 49. How dare she!*

While I was screaming at her in my mind, I smiled weakly and thanked her. I could feel the redness of embarrassment creep up my neck, over my face, and even into my scalp, which was concealed by my white hair. That did it for shopping that day. I took my old, exercised body and slinked into my rental car. The four-door Lincoln *did* look old-lady-ish. I wanted to shout that I had a car-rental discount coupon, not based on age, for a two-level upgrade. I really should have been driving a Mustang!

The clerk in the store didn't mean to insult me. She was giving me an added discount on merchandise. But, I felt both wounded and outraged.

17

Talking About Menopause

After that experience, I realized how sensitive I would need to be to the women I approached for interviews for a book on menopause. As I made those approaches, I was pleasantly surprised. The first women I talked to were so enthusiastic that I decided to try another idea. I asked women if they would be willing to be interviewed in focus groups of approximately the same age range.

The first group met during lunchtime. (They all worked.) I was amazed at the openness. Nobody wanted to stop at the end of the hour. I found myself greatly encouraged and less anxious about some of my own symptoms and feelings. Other women had experienced the same things. They were able to laugh, talk, and offer suggestions. The atmosphere was warm and relaxing, exactly the opposite of what I had anticipated.

> *There is a time for everything, and a season for every activity under heaven.*
> *—Ecclesiastes 3:1 (NIV)*

After that first one, all the groups met in women's homes. When the research was completed, a few of the groups decided to continue to meet as support groups. The setting was safe, and the stories from other women were comforting.

The silence seemed to be over, and women were ready to talk. That openness continues today; in fact, it is growing. Every October 18, World Menopause Day is celebrated by women who intend to raise awareness of the issues connected with menopause. The World Health Organization says that 1.1 billion women will be age 50 or over by 2005. Many of these women will benefit from this growing awareness.

A Word of Encouragement

Menopause happens to each woman blessed to reach this age. Our generation and those following are further blessed with newfound information. This, and a touch of wisdom, enhances the way we move through this life passage.

Remember that God designed our bodies to make this change; it's a natural part of aging. While it necessitates adjustment, it also brings new insights, freedom, and fresh perspectives. Even though there were times when I wished I were elsewhere, this life stage isn't *all* bad.

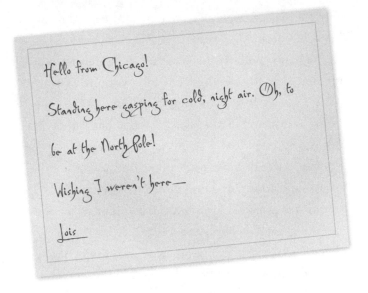

Hello from Chicago!

Standing here gasping for cold, night air. Oh, to

be at the North Pole!

Wishing I weren't here—

Lois

CHAPTER 2

Hot and Cold and All Shook Up

One of the hallmarks of menopause is the variety and unpredictability of symptoms. Some women experience very few symptoms, others experience them all— sometimes at the same time.

Hot Flashes and Night Sweats

Hot flashes and night sweats are two of the most common symptoms of menopause, with an estimated 75 to 85 percent of menopausal women suffering from them. They are actually the same symptom, differentiated by when they occur. *Night sweats* happen in the middle of the night, interrupting sleep. *Hot flashes* happen during waking hours. Both last longer than an instant but usually not more than five minutes. The most definitive element of these symptoms is their unpredictability.

Drs. Sharon and David Sneed describe hot flashes this way in their book, *Prime Time*: "The flushes are extremely unpredictable, occurring with varying frequency, intensity, and duration. They are usually described as a sudden, uncomfortable feeling of intense warmth in the face, neck, and chest."[1]

Hot flashes and night sweats are related to decreasing levels of estrogen in the body, but little is known as to why a drop in estrogen sets off these reactions. Utian and Jacobowitz describe what is known about hot flashes:

> What we do know, however, is that when estrogen production drops abruptly during the perimenopause [the years prior to the cessation of a woman's period], there is a change in the brain's chemistry that affects the temperature control center in the hypothalamus. The result is a decrease in the body's core temperature set point that triggers dilation of the blood vessels of the skin and sweating as the body attempts to reset its thermostat.[2]

Although hot flashes are not dangerous, they can be embarrassing. Others may not seem to notice a woman's dripping appearance anywhere near as much as the woman thinks they do, but a woman suffering a hot flash feels exposed.

And a lack of notice does not mean that a woman is exaggerating the degree of heat she feels and the amount of perspiration her body is producing. Perhaps others who are with a woman experiencing a hot flash don't notice for two reasons: (1) we are too self-absorbed to look carefully at others, and (2) people perspire at all ages. It is considered a rather normal body function and draws little attention.

Hot flashes are certainly a disturbing symptom of menopause. They reinforce a sense of being out of control over your own body, and they disrupt normal life. But they don't last forever—it just feels that way.

Hot-Flash Stories

I have experienced only one bona fide hot flash. There was no premonition of impending calamity. Life was going along as usual. I was in my early forties and felt great. My plan to age without evidence was working.

I had been on a speaking trip to the east coast and was coming back home by way of Chicago. I took advantage of the layover to visit a girlfriend. She and I were eating a wonderfully elegant dinner in a well-known downtown restaurant. I was just digging into a decadent chocolate-chocolate dessert when *it* happened. Sweat started to pour out of my skin. I gasped with fear and the need for air. I pulled the collar of my blouse away from my neck and felt a rush of tropical steam blast my face. My friend was unaware of my hysteria, her attention fully given to her own chocolate-chocolate dessert.

Panic seized me as I realized that this was not stopping. I slammed the palms of my hands against the edge of the table and bolted without explanation to my friend. The first breath of relief came as I burst out the front door of the restaurant into the middle of the busy Chicago sidewalk. The doorman evidently had seen this kind of behavior before, for he simply smiled politely as I hung onto the awning pole sucking in the cold night air.

I was still standing there drawing in air and puffing steam when my confused friend found me.

"What is happening?" she asked with puzzled concern.

"I am so *hot*!" I yelled. I could breathe now, but the residual heat from my first hot flash was still seeping out of my shaking body.

My friend looked at me with an expression of dismay as she shivered in the wintry cold. I was only forty-two, but she was a mere youth of thirty. I didn't realize that I had experienced a hot flash; she didn't even know what a hot flash was.

I am grateful (though mystified as to why) that I have not experienced that particular pandemonium again. Most women who suffer from hot flashes are not so blessed. Their first one is usually followed by an unpredictable series of body-thermostat failures.

In one of my focus groups, Marge told us about surviving a particularly public episode. She is a beautiful blond in her late forties who loves to wear luscious silk dresses. She is meticulous—never a wrinkle, certainly never a perspiration stain. Her first hot flash happened in church on Easter.

"We were sitting near the front, of course," she told the group. "I had on a pale blue silk dress and all of a sudden, I was sweating. My dress started to stick to my skin—everywhere! My hair was stuck to my head. I looked like someone had poured a bucket of water over me. It was awful. There was nowhere to go, no way to sneak out. I was drenched from the skin out," she said, able to smile now at the recollection.

Then Betty spoke up. She said she didn't know if she had ever had a hot flash or not. The response was unanimous.

"If you don't know, then you haven't had one."

A hot flash is far more than a feeling of being very hot. I lived in Florida for thirteen years and I was very hot most of the time. Just going from an air-conditioned house to an air-conditioned car was enough time, in the sultry south-Florida heat, for your whole body to break out in a sweat. But, as hot as that experience was, it was *not* like a hot flash.

Perspiration as a result of the weather is your body's response to an external change. A hot flash is your body's response to an internal change. The heat starts deep inside and surges through the body, finally exploding through the pores of the skin. The feeling is one of being cooked all the way through. It is common to be consumed by a need for cool air and panicked at the suddenness and intensity of what is happening.

Some women respond in dramatic ways, as Ann shared with her group.

"I have a friend who was at a party—crowded, hot, stuffy—and had such a bad hot flash that she ran into the bathroom and ripped off her clothes." Ann's friend spent several minutes there naked, trying to compose herself. After cooling down, she put her soggy clothes back on, combed her damp hair, and rejoined the party.

Carol had hot flashes that worsened when she was caring for her sick father. "The stress was incredible. My body went nuts. Things got better after I was out from under so much stress."

Allison said that the thing she hated most about her hot flashes was the blinding sensation and dizziness that preceded them.

"I was at lunch the other day with a woman I had just met. It was a business lunch, so I wanted to be fairly coherent. We were sitting at the table talking when everything dimmed. I had this moment of dizziness and knew what was coming. My vision cleared quickly, but then the water started to pour. I took my suit jacket off, hoping she didn't know why. The dizziness also was gone almost right away, but the sweat just wouldn't quit. My colleague graciously didn't comment. How could she have missed my suddenly drenched appearance?"

A Bedtime Tale

All of these women experienced numerous hot flashes over varying periods of time. Many of them spent many sleepless nights because the drenchings also occurred in the dark.

26

Amy lives in the air-conditioned comfort of her lovely Florida home. As she entered her mid-forties she started to experience hot flashes during the day and night sweats during the night. She kept lowering the thermostat, but that didn't help. While she was burning up, using no covers at all, her husband complained that he was freezing under a pile of blankets. She slept in absorbent cotton nightgowns as recommended. But she still was drenched night after night.

Barbara's husband had leg pains that he felt actually were brought on by the temperature in the bedroom. Kim's problem was exhaustion, "The night sweats keep me awake most of the night."

Sleep that knits up the ravelled sleave [sic] of care, The death of each day's life, sore labour's bath, Balm of the hurt minds, great nature's second course, Chief nourisher in life's feast.
—William Shakespeare

Suggestions for Survival

HRT was probably the most popular treatment for menopausal symptoms. That ended when the results of the Women's Health Initiative (WHI) were published in July 2002. Further evidence against HRT use has caused many women to search for non-hormonal remedies for their symptoms, particularly hot flashes and night sweats.

One natural remedy for relief of hot flashes is vitamin E. The dosage can vary with each woman, but the range is usually between a total of 400 IU and 1200 IU a day. Women with liver disease should check with their doctors before taking vitamin E.

There are some indications that hot flashes and night sweats may also be linked to blood-sugar imbalance. In Linda Ojeda's book *Menopause Without Medicine,* she points out this correlation between women who experience hot flashes and the possibility of a blood-sugar imbalance, or hypoglycemia. She suggests, "If your first menopausal symptom is a hot flash, consider: How many of the known triggers of both hot flashes and hypoglycemia—caffeine, alcohol, heavily spiced foods, sugar, and so on—are a normal part of your diet?"[3]

The women interviewed in the focus groups confirmed that hot flashes and night sweats are highly individualistic symptoms, and successful therapies are equally individualistic. Some women found almost immediate relief with HRT. Others noticed a change simply with increased dosages of vitamin E. Controlled diets helped others. And, for some, nothing seemed to help.

If hot flashes and night sweats are relentless, even after attempting several therapies, living with them is the only alternative. Women who have been in this unpredictable predicament share some practical advice.

- Wear nightgowns and underwear made of 100 percent cotton instead of nylon or other nonabsorbent materials.
- If you are in an enclosed place like an office building when a hot flash occurs, get some fresh air

as soon as possible. Excuse yourself and go outside for a few moments.

- Keep a glass of cool water handy and sip on it. This won't prevent a hot flash, but it can help to cool down your body.

- If you are going to be away from home all day, carry a change of underwear. At least after the hot flash ends, you can change into something dry. Some women even keep an extra blouse with them.

- If a hot flash occurs while you are around other people, slip off by yourself for a few moments and simply relax. Breathe deeply and slowly, take a drink of water, and give your body an opportunity to calm down.

Sooner or later all women will stop having periods, but it is uncommon for them to stop abruptly, neatly, or in a predictable pattern.

Irregular Periods

I have carried a daily planner for about 20 years. Without it, I don't know where I am or where I am supposed to be. In my month-at-a-glance pages, I always lightly penciled in a circle around the date of my next expected period. I had never been off by more than two days until age 45. During menopause, I still penciled in those circles, but I used an eraser much more often, since my periods were so unpredictable.

Sooner or later all women will stop having periods, but it is uncommon for them to stop abruptly, neatly, or in a predictable pattern. It is much more common for women to have irregular periods before complete cessation occurs.

Missed periods are no cause for alarm, except for the possibility of an unexpected pregnancy. (Of all the women I interviewed, none of them had an unexpected pregnancy during the process of menopause.) In general, after a woman's period has ceased for a year, she is usually considered to have completed menopause and is no longer able to conceive a child. If you do not want a child at this stage of life, be sure to practice birth control of some kind until your doctor has declared you past your reproductive years. This can be determined by a simple blood test that registers hormone levels.

Increased bleeding, on the other hand, is cause for alarm. This can be dangerous and demands immediate attention. Frequent bleeding takes several forms: spotting, more frequent periods, bleeding between regular periods, heavier and/or longer periods, and hemorrhaging.

In *Menopause and the Years Ahead,* Mary Beard and Lindsay Curtis explain what is happening when bleeding—spotting to hemorrhaging—occurs during menopause:

> Spotting is common during menopause because of decreasing estrogen production by the ovaries. When ovulation fails to occur because of the diminishing number of ova, the lining in your uterus continues to thicken until it reaches the point where it begins to fragment. At this point, irregular and often unpredictable bleeding occurs.[4]

They go on to caution that any abnormal bleeding should be checked by a doctor. There is usually nothing to worry about, but seeing a doctor is good preventive medicine: Increased bleeding can be a sign of cancer.

I have already recounted my frightening first experience with hemorrhaging. In all the books I have since read on menopause, there was very little said about more frequent bleeding except the consistent warning to check with your doctor. But I also wanted the comfort of hearing from or about other women who had experienced this problem. What I didn't find in books, I found in interviews.

Many women had similar war stories of heavy bleeding. Perhaps women had been hesitant to talk about this symptom because it is so embarrassing. It is a situation that women feel they should be able to handle on their own. There is an attitude that, certainly by her mid-forties, a woman

Determining Blood Flow

If you are experiencing excessive blood flow, it is important that you explain this to your doctor in ways that help him or her gauge just how much blood you are losing. Monitor how many pads or tampons you saturate in a given time period. Since the absorbencies for tampons are standard industry-wide, note which "strength" of tampon you are using and how many grams it holds. If this is an ongoing problem, keep a diary that describes the degree of saturation and the frequency with which you must change your protection.

should be able to dress fastidiously, function with calm, and handle the logistics of her period without outside help. In the privacy of the group interviews, though, women readily expressed the discomfort and fear they felt about bleeding, and they agreed they would not have felt so overwhelmed if they had known that other women suffered the same thing.

Hemorrhaging is the most dramatic form of heavy bleeding. As with hot flashes, if you must ask for a definition, you probably have not experienced it. For the uninitiated, it often means that you cannot be out in public because you cannot prevent bleeding through all protection and onto your clothes.

Hemorrhaging usually requires medical attention because the bleeding can be heavy enough to cause anemia, a reduced amount of red blood cells. In extreme cases, fainting and hypovolemic shock (shock due to extreme blood loss) can occur.[5]

Alarming as all of this sounds, hemorrhaging is considered to be within the range of "normal" for menopausal woman, but it should not be dismissed. A woman experiencing this problem should seek medical attention so that her doctor can treat the cause and thereby relieve the bleeding. The following stories give examples of the help that is possible.

Debbie

Debbie is a manager in a large corporation. She is a petite blond who smiles a lot and is known for her encouraging personality. Her easy-going manner endears

Date: _____

These were my particular decisions about treatment and how I came to these decisions ...

her to just about everyone and gives the impression that nothing much ruffles her feathers.

But, Debbie now has an ongoing challenge to her ability to remain unruffled, as she has recurrent bouts of hemorrhaging. They began when she was in her mid-forties. She started flooding at night. Then, instances began to happen in the daytime. A dilatation and curettage (D and C) revealed no traces of cancer and temporarily cleared up the condition. But the hemorrhaging resumed after a few months. As Debbie recounted, she might be out dining with her husband and friends when the hemorrhaging would hit. After several trips to the ladies' room, she and her husband would have to leave so she could go home and get off her feet. When that did not relieve the bleeding, she would head to the doctor's office again.

Debbie has had biopsies to rule out cancer, but she continues to live with the unexpected disruption of hemorrhaging. To regulate her hormones and reduce the bleeding, her doctor put her on and took her off birth control pills for six months at a time. This regimen has seemed to help.

Eileen

Eileen was in line for the submarine ride at Walt Disney World when she had her first hemorrhage.

"They [staff at Disney World] took me to the clinic where they suggested I go to a doctor," she recounted. "I went back to my hotel room and saw a doctor later."

She rested the remainder of the day and the bleeding slowed down. It was a frightening and embarrassing experience for her, but it was not abnormal. Eileen went to her doctor and verified that the bleeding was not from a cancerous condition, and she needed no further treatment.

Linda

Linda was actually in the doctor's office when the hemorrhaging began. "At least I was in a place where I could get immediate help!" she said. She tried HRT but still had some bleeding problems, and she finally had a hysterectomy to remedy the excessive bleeding.

Partnership with Your Doctor

The reason so many warnings are given about abnormal bleeding is because it can be a sign of endometrial cancer. Drs. Winnifred B. Cutler and Celso-Ramón García define endrometrial cancer this way:

> Your endometrium is a gland that lines the central cavity of the uterus. The endometrium grows and thickens with each menstrual cycle, finally sloughing off during the menstrual flow. This tissue sometimes develops an overgrowth (a condition called endometrial hyperplasia), or, rarely, evolves into the more diseased state—the cancer.[6]

The prospect of cancer is frightening, but for those who have verified the cause of their abnormal bleeding with their doctor—take courage. In his book *1250 Health-Care Questions Women Ask*, Dr. Joe S. McIlhaney, Jr. explains that irregular bleeding during menopause usually does not persist month after month:

> Most women who have abnormal bleeding worry about the cause being cancer, especially if it occurs when they are forty or over. It is important that a woman realize, however, that the cause of such bleeding is not usually cancer.

> Remember, cancer is basically a "sore." As it grows it begins oozing a little fluid and then a little blood. Then, as time passes— perhaps weeks and months—that sore begins oozing more and more blood. This pattern of bleeding is quite different from the sporadic episodes of bleeding that almost all women occasionally have. The real key, though, is whether abnormal uterine bleeding is persisting.[7]

I had lain awake nights worrying that my irregular bleeding was a sign of cancer, so it was a great relief to get the results of the D and C and biopsy to find out that this was not cancer. But when I was going through those first frightening episodes, I wish I had known that these are often a normal part of menopause.

Some women will not go for diagnostic testing because they are afraid of the results. They hope all is well and go on. But ignoring the possibility of cancer is gambling unnecessarily with your own health.

If you have abnormal bleeding, call your doctor's office for an appointment. Your doctor will probably perform an endometrial biopsy, which is done in the office, usually without anesthesia. The doctor will snip a tiny sampling of tissue from the lining of the uterus. That sampling is examined in a laboratory to determine if any of the cells are abnormal.

I have had an endometrial biopsy and found it untraumatic. There was an uncomfortable sensation for about ten seconds, and that was all. One woman interviewed, however, found it very painful and had resultant cramps. Discuss the possibility of anesthesia with your doctor if pain is a concern.

When considering treatment, discuss your options and concerns in detail with your doctor.

In the case of hemorrhaging, your doctor may want to do a D and C. That procedure allows for laboratory examination of cells, and it usually clears up abnormal bleeding. It may also be done in the doctor's office with local anesthesia or in the hospital. Again, it depends on the individual.

As I said earlier, I had a D and C in the doctor's office and experienced minimal discomfort. Other women I spoke with were admitted to the hospital for D and Cs, which enabled them to have general anesthesia.

When considering treatment, discuss your options and concerns in detail with your doctor. If you are more comfortable in the hospital under general anesthesia, allow yourself to express that preference. Be sure that you have an honest, trusting relationship with your doctor, and do what you agree is best for you.

Suggestions for Survival

Sometimes, irregular bleeding persists even if you have a D and C. Reasons for this vary. You and your doctor can discuss your options, which may include a hysterectomy to end this particular symptom permanently. If you do not choose that route, here are other suggestions to make it through rough times:

- See your doctor.
- Have diagnostic testing done.
- Carry tampons with you at all times.
- Record the dates of your periods and episodes of bleeding. This will help you and your doctor evaluate your symptoms.
- Talk to other women for encouragement.

A Word of Encouragement

The number of possible symptoms of menopause can seem overwhelming. But remember … every woman who lives past mid-life experiences this life passage. The symptoms are not always severe, there is help to manage them well, and they do eventually cease.

There is a blessing, too, that we don't experience these symptoms while we are raising young families. Our childbearing years are past, and now we are better able, by virtue of circumstances and experience, to "teach the young women" (Titus 2:4 KJV).

Hello from the peaks and valleys of emotions—
I've plopped down in the middle of my sunroom—
crying. I'm a mess, a jangled mess. Aerobics and
endorphins just aren't cutting it.
Wishing I weren't here—

Lois

CHAPTER 3

Mind, Waist, and Emotions— What Next?

Now where was I? Oh yes, memory!

I began each one of my interview groups by asking the women how old they were. In one particular group, each woman wrote the information down on a piece of paper except for Elaine, who was fishing around in her purse.

I offered her paper and a pencil, but she said, "Oh, no, I'm looking for my pocket calculator."

"Your calculator?" I asked. The room became quiet.

"Yes," she said, still fumbling. "I can't remember how old I am. I can remember the year, but not how old I am now."

Elaine sensed all eyes turn on her. She looked up from her bottomless purse. She saw traces of smiles appear and knew she had said something amusing.

"What?" she asked, smiling as well.

"Did you say you *forgot* your own age?" someone asked.

We laughed. The familiar symptom of memory loss had been demonstrated and the evening had only just begun.

Memory Loss

Everybody experiences memory loss to one degree or another, but the kind associated with menopause is short-term memory loss. Dr. Wulf Utian explains it this way: "Recently, decreasing estrogen levels were linked to changes in short-term memory. The ability to remember immediate events, like the items on your shopping list, or to recall where you left your car keys or sunglasses can be attributed to declining estrogen levels."[1]

On a trip to California some years ago, I had an exaggerated experience of this kind. I was staying with my older daughter in San Diego before driving up to Pasadena to speak at a conference. The morning I departed, I was the last one to leave Lisa's apartment. She and her husband had already gone to work, and I was enjoying a leisurely morning.

I made several trips to load my car. After checking the apartment to make sure I hadn't left anything, I locked the apartment door and hid the key in the designated spot. I slid into my rental car, put the key in the ignition, and then stopped.

Did I lock the door ... or just hide the key? I asked myself.

I got out of the car and went back to the apartment. The door was locked. Back to the car.

I sat down, put the key in the ignition, and stopped again. *Had I locked the door?*

I got out of the car and went back to the apartment. The door was locked. Back to the car.

A third time the same doubt came over me. *Had I locked the door?*

This time I was able to overcome the urge to go back and check the door for the third time—*but not because I remembered locking it.* I felt absolutely ridiculous. I pictured someone watching me from an apartment window. They were probably dialing the local mental hospital to report an amnesic lady on the loose.

In one of the focus groups, Gail related how her memory loss had impacted her reading. "I love to read, but I haven't in the last year because I can't concentrate." She couldn't remember enough to follow a plot from one night to the next.

Several other women described this loss of memory as "fogginess" or "fuzzy brain." The sensation is one of clouded thinking; it takes a moment to call up information that used to be accessed quite easily.

"I was in a store the other day and the clerk asked me for my previous address. I couldn't remember the name of the street," Tammy said. Eventually she was able to pull the name up from her scrambled memory bank, but she described her brain as feeling fuzzy the whole time.

Interestingly enough, these women function well at the office. Remembering complex data doesn't seem to be a problem—unlike remembering what they had done thirty seconds ago or recalling a fact they've known for years.

Aids for an Ailing Memory

Some women report improved memory when they begin taking HRT. Others remember more accurately when they add vitamin B_1 to their diet.

Of course, the most obvious aid for compensating for memory loss is to write things down. I take notes religiously. I adopted this practice 23 years ago when my husband died in a hot-air balloon accident. My memory became suddenly overtaxed as I had to close his business and raise two girls alone. List making became an integral part of my life.

My planner is jammed with all kinds of notes to myself. Disorganized as it looks, I can find what I need instantly. I am amused when I see planners that record only appointments, for mine has detailed lists of each day's activities. But my memory is pretty deficient! You may only need a simple list to compensate for the temporary memory deficiency that occurs during menopause.

Where Is My Waist?

I was sitting in the living room of a lovely California home, listening to one woman after another express her frustration over the additional ten pounds (or more) that she could not shed. As one woman was talking about her expanding waist, a loud "pop" interrupted her. Another woman's belt had burst open—a graphic visual aid of an annoying symptom of menopause.

I was blessed with a metabolism that allowed me to eat whatever I wanted until I hit forty. No one warned me that metabolism changes at mid-life. I kept eating as usual, but I started to gain weight. Like so many other women, most of it was hanging around my waist.

Utian and Jacobowitz explain this metabolism change in *Managing Your Menopause*:

> Beginning in your mid-thirties, and compounded by menopause, which usually begins in your early fifties, your food intake needs to be scaled back to accommodate your slower metabolism. Nature has rigged our basal metabolic rate (BMR) to slow down after the age of twenty-five, sliding between one-half and one percent per year. It happens gradually, so that it may be some time before you realize that you can't eat the way you once did. If you continue to consume the same amount of food that you have in the past, you will have difficulty keeping your figure.[2]

One woman commented on the irony of the situation, "Isn't it unfair? Most of us as kids were picky eaters. Then you grow up and you want to eat more, and [your] metabolism changes."

Weight gain is a physical symptom that isn't painful technically, but it can cause distress in a number of ways.

You don't feel good about yourself if you are dissatisfied with your appearance. If you choose to forget about weighing what you did at 30, you have to adjust to your new body weight—and shape. One woman said she couldn't get used to her new body. She gained fourteen pounds during her forties and couldn't seem to lose it. She accepted her new look; but having been thin to begin with, she felt as if she no longer understood her own body.

Suggestions for Survival

Memory loss and weight gain are frustrating symptoms of menopause. In addition to a new planning notebook and a new belt, here are some things to think about when trying to live with these two changes:

- Remember—memory loss is normal and does not last forever.
- Be willing to use aids, like planning calendars and lists, without guilt. Many busy people with excellent memories use both.
- Try to reduce the level of stress in your life. Too much activity can result in memory overload.
- Be aware of the potential change in your body metabolism.
- Begin to train yourself to investigate healthy eating habits.
- Go ahead and buy clothes that fit. If you squeeze back into clothing that is too tight, you'll only feel guilty and depressed.

- Refer often to chapter 7, which discusses diet and exercise.
- Uh, I forget the last one. But that's okay.

Emotional State of "Otherness"

Women who suffer from unstable emotions during menopause have a tough battle, given the perceptions associated with this symptom and the degree to which they may suffer.

"Take my hormones away, and I'll kill!" one otherwise rational woman said in the middle of a focus group. Of course, she was kidding—sort of. She had experienced such severe emotional distress during menopause that she was hospitalized at one point for psychiatric evaluation. HRT corrected this problem for her, and now she guards her hormones with vitriolic fervor.

Emotional distress is what doctors of old stereotyped as the "hysterical female" syndrome. This symptom caused many menopausal women to be swept off to mental institutions and declared insane. It was thought to spring from the mind, having no physiological basis.

I have a friend in Florida whose mother committed suicide at age 55 (some forty-seven years ago) because no one could help her out of her depression. She had been fine until her early fifties, and then she changed suddenly. My friend attributes his mother's changed personality and subsequent suicide to undiagnosed menopause. He remembers his mother

Memory is the thing you forget with.
—Alexander Chase

before she changed. He does not believe she could have "just gone mad."

Fortunately, society's attitudes are changing. Emotional distress—manifested as anxiety, depression, irritability, and crying spells—has been studied and linked to the decrease of estrogen production.

Dr. Raymond G. Burnett, in his book *Menopause: All Your Questions Answered,* writes about this connection between decreased estrogen and emotional distress during the years prior to a woman's last period (the *perimenopausal* years).

> Many excellent studies now indicate that low levels of estrogen occurring in the perimenopausal years do have a definite physiological effect on important centers in the brain. In addition to hot flashes, the "withdrawal" from estrogen causes changes in the brain, which affect a woman's thought processes and lead to depression, anxiety, irritability, forgetfulness, insomnia, crying spells, lethargy, and fatigue. These are not symptoms of the woman who is ill-prepared for the menopause or the symptoms of a psychologically weak person. They are hormonally caused and have a physiological basis.[3]

Trapped in an Alien Body

I have always been emotional. Just ask my daughters or my husband. "Mom cries at the playing of the national anthem at a football game," my daughters attest. "She even cries at the photos of dogs up for adoption in the newspaper. She's afraid they won't find a good home."

My emotions can certainly be effusive, but they are not the kind that lead to anxiety or depression. When I feel bad, I express myself openly, and the feelings of anger or frustration are over quickly. Lingering negative feelings are just not part of my personality.

Or they weren't … until about age 45.

Out of the blue, I experienced several "attacks" of feeling jangled, fragmented, anxious—totally unrelated to circumstances. Perhaps the best way to describe one of these attacks is to include the following journal entry.

> *Out of the blue, I experienced several "attacks" of feeling jangled, fragmented, anxious— totally unrelated to circumstances.*

Tuesday, November 9, 1993

I am undone. My nerves are jangled. I feel like someone took an egg beater—or a food processor—and surged through my insides. I don't feel sick, nauseated, physically unwell. But I AM NOT MYSELF. I am not even the "self" of me that is emotionally gushing. This is different. It is like being trapped in an alien body. What is happening? I have never felt this way in the past (prior to this last year). Even in times of great trauma in the past, I have been able to cope. I have been able to quiet my spirit before the Lord and go on. Now I am rattled, a mess.

Just this morning, I got out my at-home aerobic exercise step and started to exercise. I prayed that the endorphins would kick in quickly and I would start to feel better. After thirty minutes of action-packed determination, I started to cry. Undaunted by the inconvenience of tears mingled with sweat, I kept on for another ten minutes. No good. Endorphins or not, I still felt like I just couldn't manage my body.

I pulled a chair into a sunny circle of the sunroom and sat down before the Lord. A heap. I was a heap. Sweating, crying, shaking—Lord, please help me. I knew that the Lord was with me. But no amount of spiritual fervor could take away the physical reality of dramatic changes going on inside my body. It was as if I had spigots inside me being turned on and off rapidly, releasing and cutting off some well-being fluid. I did not feel abandoned by the Lord, but I felt that a lot of things were going on that He intended to allow to continue. After a few minutes of crying out to Him, I called my doctor.

I explained how I felt to my doctor's nurse and that I had my daughter's wedding coming up in December and wanted to be semi-coherent for the big event. The nurse was wonderful—kind and reassuring. She promised me she would talk to my doctor and call back quickly. She did call back within twenty minutes and told me the doctor prescribed hormones for me to try until after the wedding, and then we could reevaluate. Thank God. I am in such bad shape, I long for relief. Where is the old me? Where is the survivor? Deluged or dehydrated by the ebb and flow of internal controllers.

And so, I ask myself, if women who read this book want to know how these waves of

These were my experiences that (I believe) resulted from my treatment choices …

Date: _____

Postcards from Menopause: Wishing I Weren't Here Copyright © 2003 FamilyLife. All rights reserved. www.familylife.com

"otherness" differ from emotional upsets in the past, what would I say? I would say that the main difference is that my methods for coping in difficult circumstances or during emotional upheaval don't work. Even on the worst emotional roller-coaster rides, I have never felt unable to grasp onto truth in a way that calms the emotions. Now, I am aware of the truth, but my body keeps me unwillingly on this scary ride. My faith and beliefs are intact, but the gears that slow down the roller coaster are disengaged. I pull the same levers, but the ride only speeds up.

This is about coping. I have often been called a survivor, so this inability to cope with feelings makes me mad. I want to rise above the circumstances. I want to will my body to behave. I want to trust that the Lord will give me that amazing grace to which I have become so accustomed. It is not about faith. I have talked to many Christian women who have felt guilty because their faith could not get them through this passage of life without medical help. Faith is not measured by accepting assistance for stress versus gutting it out on your own. Help comes in many forms. For women in hormonal stress, one of the ways help comes is through hormone replacement therapy. It is not the only way, but it is a way that is as acceptable to the faith-filled believer as it is for anyone else.

Please note that at the time I wrote this, the medical community considered HRT safe and effective. In chapter 4, I explain how this is no longer the case.

Hysterectomies and Emotions

Almost one-third of the women I interviewed (31 out of 105) had undergone hysterectomies. A hysterectomy may or may not include removal of the ovaries. If it does, the production of estrogen in the body is stopped abruptly. Of the women I interviewed, those who had their ovaries removed, but were not put on hormones immediately, experienced severe emotional ups and downs. The sudden absence of estrogen caused this.

Naomi said, "I woke from the surgery and felt out of control. I was crying uncontrollably. It was like watching myself go nuts. This young girl was pushing me from one room to another in a wheelchair and she kept bumping me into things. I started screaming and crying."

For Naomi, the waves of emotional irrationality continued. She asked her doctor about them, and he said it was all in her mind. He told her that her body had healed, but her mind had not. His insensitive manner propelled Naomi into another frenzy. It also propelled her to seek the advice of another doctor. Her new doctor put her on HRT, and within a few weeks Naomi was back to normal.

Emotions That Are Difficult to Define

Among the women interviewed, even the most emotional ones agreed that menopausal emotions were different from what they usually experienced.

"I just don't feel myself," Ann said. "I feel emotionally out of control. I feel fragmented."

On an intellectual level, reason prevails—during emotional distress, most women are aware that their feelings are hormonally induced. Yet, their intellects are held captive by emotions. They feel frightened by their loss of control. It was apparent in the conversations that words fall short of adequately describing this distressing symptom.

Further Sources of Distress

During menopause, a woman may think that *all* of her emotional distresses result from fluctuating hormones. But other factors may be involved. At this life stage, children leave home for work or college. A woman who has waited to start a family may suddenly realize that time has run out. Or she may find herself assuming the role of caregiver to her aging parents.

Even without the influence of hormones, this time of life is full of difficult changes—all of which affect emotions. Just realizing that these changes are a natural part of life—aside from menopause—can be a great relief.

That Elusive Sense of Well-Being

"I don't have real discernible mood swings," Lynn said when asked about emotional distress, "but I have noticed a general sense of free-floating anxiety. In the last few years, I just seem to be a little anxious, a little apprehensive, like something bad is going to happen."

Lynn is not alone. Many women express the same sense of general anxiety. They may not feel out of control, but a once-routine sense of well-being is missing.

I felt this to some degree. It manifested as a return to that "future-is-uncertain" feeling I remembered from my high-school years. That had ended in my thirties, when I felt I had stopped flitting around in life and had reached a peaceful plateau. But in menopause, the flitting feeling came back. It was not constant and not always severe.

These periods of uneasiness are never welcome, but hormone fluctuations alone are not always to blame. There are seasons when the future *is* uncertain, and mid-life is one of those. Later on I'll share how some unsettling circumstances often coincide with mid-life. But the elusive sense of well-being I'm talking about here is less connected to the circumstances of objective reality than it is to free-floating, unpredictable angst.

Suggestions for Survival

Women going through menopause are *not* crazy. Although in earlier times women were often misdiagnosed and institutionalized, there is no need to fear such extreme reactions. Today, there is help. Following are some ways to help you stabilize emotions:

- Take time away from the hustle and bustle of everyday life, even if it means excusing yourself from the height of an activity.

- Increase your spiritual intake. We'll look at this more closely in chapter 12.

- Evaluate the level of stress in your life, and try to lessen stress factors.

- Talk with other women for encouragement and hope.

• Find a doctor who will work with you in ways that are affirming to you.

Fatigue

"I used to be a night person," Elaine said, "and now I start to nod off around nine o'clock. My husband can be sitting reading or watching television, and I fall asleep sitting up."

Elaine occasionally has night sweats that interrupt her sleep. Fatigue is a predictable result. Other women in her focus group experienced increased fatigue and attributed it to changes in their metabolisms. Endless energy and that after-dinner second burst of steam are things of the past. Since the onset of menopause, they feel lethargic, and a slower metabolism has caused weight gain and decreased energy.

> *Weeping may remain for a night, but rejoicing comes in the morning.*
> *—Psalm 30:5*

"I feel weighted down," Mary said. "I eat the same as I used to, but [I] have gained weight and, as a result, [I] feel more tired."

Women reported that reducing calorie intake, resting or napping more frequently, and exercising helped them minimize their fatigue.

Dizziness

Dizziness is another side effect of menopause. Some women said they experienced dizziness at the beginning of a hot flash. Others had bouts with dizziness and no accompanying hot flashes.

53

In general, dizzy spells last only a few seconds and are not debilitating. If you feel dizzy, sit and wait for the feeling to pass. Get up slowly and take your time moving around. Usually, the sensation is corrected with a few minutes of rest. If dizziness persists or is severe, see a doctor. He should check you to rule out other causes.

Loss of Libido and Vaginal Dryness

Some women experience changes in their sexual desires. Unlike the supposed oversexed, hysterical, menopausal female of history, some of the women I interviewed lost interest in sex during menopause. They attributed their change in desire to fatigue, emotional ups and downs, hot flashes, and vaginal dryness.

> *Unlike the supposed oversexed, hysterical, menopausal female of history, some of the women I interviewed lost interest in sex during menopause.*

This last symptom was one that women in the focus groups rarely discussed openly. Rather, they came to me privately to admit that they had a decreased interest in sex.

In one such case, an attractive, vivacious woman confessed that she hated to admit her lack of interest openly because it contradicted how she had enjoyed her sexual relationship with her husband before menopause. Cures have evaded her. Because of a strong family history of breast cancer, she could not take HRT. No other treatment, like vitamins or diet changes, seemed to help.

54

She and her husband were talking honestly with each other, and she underscored that this was a symptom of menopause—not rejection. Fortunately he believed her and was willing to work with her on ways to restore intimacy.

At this writing, great passion hasn't returned. But their loving relationship allows for sexual expression that is less frequent—but still meaningful.

The restoration of intimacy is important to husbands and wives alike, and bringing back that vitality often takes effort from both parties. In my conversations about this delicate issue, the adjustments that women suggested could very well involve husbands, too. Some women said that relieving other menopausal symptoms—particularly stress and fatigue—helped to restore their interest in sex. Reducing those factors involves changes to home and habits—which will likely affect the expectations of those in the household. They also said that weekend trips or getaways with their husbands helped.

In our conversations, the women also emphasized overall lifestyle. They agreed that taking care of themselves helped them feel attractive. That confidence helped rekindle old flames of desire that had been extinguished with the multitude of changes during menopause.

Another complicating factor to intimacy had little to do with desire. Those who experienced vaginal dryness said they didn't look forward to sexual intercourse because it was painful. Estrogen creams helped some of these women, but with recent medical revelations, more women are choosing lubricating creams that do not contain hormones. A key to the effectiveness of these creams is consistent use. Coupled with the use of lubricants during intercourse, usually pain is greatly lessened and pleasure restored.

> *Memories may escape the action of the will, may sleep a long time, but when stirred by the right influence, though that influence be light as a shadow, they flash into full stature and life with everything in place.*
> —*John Muir*

A Comprehensive List

The following list includes the symptoms that have been discussed, as well as a few dozen more. They are categorized into three types: autonomic (involuntary symptoms), physical and metabolic changes, and psychogenic changes.

The word *psychogenic* means "originating in the mind or in mental conflict." This does not mean that these symptoms are some kind of mental illness. As cited earlier, there is evidence that many of these symptoms are a result of decreasing estrogen in the body. They have a physiological basis with a psychological manifestation.

This particular list is taken from *Menopause and the Years Ahead* by Mary Beard and Lindsay Curtis.

1. Autonomic (involuntary symptoms)
    hot flashes
    cold chills
    angina pectoris (chest pains)

palpitations of the heart

night sweats

increased perspiration

2. Physical and metabolic changes

menstrual changes

changes in cycle (shorten or lengthen)

changes in flow amount (increase or decrease)

breast-size decrease (atrophy)

skin thinning and wrinkling (atrophy)

vaginal atrophy (dryness, burning, itching)

discharge and occasional bleeding

dyspareunia (painful intercourse)

contracting and scarring of tissues

shortening and narrowing

vaginal relaxation with prolapsing (falling out of position)

increased facial, chest, and abdominal hair

bladder dysfunction

frequency of urination

dysuria (burning or stinging sensation when passing urine)

increased bladder infection

bladder infection symptoms without infection

osteoporosis

increased muscular weakness

        degeneration of bone joints

        increased cardiovascular disease (heart
           attacks and strokes)

3. Psychogenic

        apathy

        apprehension

        decline in libido

        depression

        fatigue

        forgetfulness

        formication (feeling like ants under the
           skin)

        frigidity

        headaches

        insomnia

        irritability

        mood changes[4]

A Word of Encouragement

After reading this list of symptoms, you may feel ready to pack your bags, head for the hills, and live in isolation. What woman wants to be around people while she is sprouting facial hair, wetting her pants, breaking her bones, forgetting her name, and scratching at the imaginary ants under her skin?

If you feel that way, remember the masses of women who preceded us. They are a testimony to survival! But since we live in an age of modern medicine, we'll look at available treatments. Chapter 5 will help you decide which ones are right for you.

Hello from the breakfast table—

*** News flash ***

The New York Times just said that HRT is worthless. What will they tell us next?

Wishing I weren't here—

Lois

CHAPTER 4

Startling Medical News

"HORMONE REPLACEMENT STUDY IS A SHOCK
TO THE MEDICAL SYSTEM"

This headline made front-page news in the *New York Times* on July 10, 2002. In fact, this study was the featured topic in dozens of newspapers across the country.

"This is the biggest bombshell that ever hit in my 30-something years in the menopause area," Dr. Wulf Utian said.[1]

Why "Bombshell"?

Women who ask this question are likely new—or uninitiated—to menopause and the controversy that has surrounded its treatment. Since the first hormone treatments for menopause were introduced in the 1930s, millions of women, according to this study, have risked their health by taking hormone replacement therapy. What is more unfortunate is that some women have taken HRT not for menopause symptoms but for protection against osteoporosis and heart disease. The July 2002 report now shows that HRT slightly *increases* the risk of heart disease. These women feel they've unwittingly traded little benefit for increased health risks.

> *This is the biggest bombshell that ever hit in my 30-something years in the menopause area.*
> *—Dr. Wulf Utian*

Dr. Utian, executive director of the North American Menopause Society and co-author of the popular 1990 book *Managing Your Menopause* was not the only one surprised by the fallout. His "bombshell" comment referred to the Women's Health Initiative, a study supported by the National Institutes of Health. The results of the study were noted in the *New York Times*. The article opened with these words:

> The announcement yesterday that a hormone replacement regimen taken by six million American women did more harm than good met with puzzlement and disbelief by women and their doctors across the country.

A rigorous study found that the drugs, a combination of estrogen and progestin, caused small increases in breast cancer, heart attacks, strokes and blood clots. Those risks outweighed the drugs' benefits—a small decrease in hip fractures and a decrease in colorectal cancer. ... In light of the findings, the study has come to a halt.[2]

Just When I Thought I'd Heard It All

More bad news came just eight months later, also reported in the *New York Times*:

"HORMONE THERAPY, ALREADY FOUND TO HAVE RISKS, IS NOW SAID TO LACK BENEFITS"

This headline ran on March 18, 2003. It brought HRT back under scrutiny and further confounded HRT users.[3] Now women who learned that HRT had actually increased their health risks were being told that HRT had little or no benefit whatsoever. The placebo comparison results pulled from that study showed that benefits related to "quality of life" were no different for women on HRT and those on placebos. The article from the *New York Times* read:

Confounding a widely held impression, a large federal study has found that hormone therapy for menopause does not affect quality of life. Women taking drugs did not feel more energetic, or have more sexual pleasure or even more restful sleep. They were not less depressed, their minds were no clearer and their memories did not appear to be improved.[4]

After reading this, I spoke with a friend of mine who had taken HRT prior to being diagnosed with breast cancer several years ago. She said, "I felt great on HRT. Now what am I supposed to think … that it was all in my head and [HRT] had no more affect than a sugar pill?"

The History and Evolution of HRT

So by now a woman might think, "I've had enough! Just tell me the best way to feel good, stay healthy, and get through this menopause thing—*and I'll do it!*"

I felt that way. It would have been easier to hear one preferred, undisputed opinion and say, "Amen. That's the route for me." But easy isn't always better, or healthier, as millions of women can testify. They took one of the most prescribed treatments, HRT, and it now proves risky.

The recent discoveries about HRT, those made since July 2002, are just a few examples of the startling risks that menopausal women have unknowingly taken in their search to relieve symptoms. A better understanding of the history of HRT (and the risks from treatment during those eras) will help women choose wisely in addressing their menopause symptoms—or any health condition, for that matter.

Estrogen's First Appearance

In the 1920s scientists linked the fluctuation of a woman's hormones with her menstrual cycle. Since her body ceased to produce estrogen after menopause, the medical community hoped that by replacing that estrogen, menopausal symptoms would be relieved. By the 1930s doctors prescribed estrogen for relief of those symptoms (with notice that FDA approval was still pending). That approval came in 1942.

This treatment, called Estrogen Replacement Therapy (ERT) was prescribed on a limited basis through the 1960s. Its use exploded upon the publication of the book *Feminine Forever* in 1965. In this book, doctor and author Robert A. Wilson made elaborate claims about the benefits of ERT. Granted, it did seem to greatly relieve menopausal symptoms. And he declared that women needed to take estrogen to remain alluring to their husbands. Though his sexist language would not win him favor with many women today, it did enrapture his '60s-era readers.

Feminine Forever

Dr. Wilson's book, *Feminine Forever,* put ERT at the top of the list of wonder cures for women. Wilson's strong language inferred that any woman who did not take estrogen was foolish. He uses the word *castration* to describe the cessation of estrogen production in the body.

Estrogen therapy was not to change a woman, Dr. Wilson insisted.

> On the contrary: *it keeps her from changing.* Therapy does not alter the natural hormone balance. Rather, it *restores* the total hormone pattern to the normal, pre-menopausal level. Whether this is interfering with nature or restoring nature is a moot point. The results speak for themselves.

> So much for the medical side of the argument. If the question is to be examined on philosophic grounds, I rest my case on the simple contention that castration is a bad thing and that every woman has the right—indeed, the duty—to counteract the chemical castration that befalls her during the middle years. Estrogen therapy is a proven, effective means of restoring the normal balance of her bodily and psychic functions throughout her prolonged life. It is nothing less than the method by which a woman can remain feminine forever.[5]

Wilson's book includes chapters entitled, "Menopause—the Loss of Womanhood and the Loss of Good Health" and "Plain Talk About Sex." In these chapters, he paints a dismal picture of a menopausal woman and appeals to the men of his day by his frank discussion of enhanced sexual relations with women who take estrogen. He discusses a "Femininity Index" which analyzes the types of vaginal cells taken by a pap smear:

> Three types of cells are visible on the slide: superficial, intermediate, and parabasal cells. The cytologist in his laboratory makes a careful count of all three cell types. This count answers one of the most crucial questions that ever confront a woman. It tells whether her body is still feminine, or whether it is gradually turning neuter.[6]

Wilson goes on to explain to husbands that if their wives are below par on the Femininity Index, estrogen will correct the problem and bring their wives' indexes up to full femininity.

These were the complications I experienced in menopause …

Date: _____

Apparently some of Wilson's medical cohorts did not approve of his strong argument for hormone replacement based on restoring women to peak sexual performance. To strengthen his case, Wilson enlisted endorsement from men in the ministry:

> Most clerics, however, have been sympathetic to my work. Knowing through their counseling work the depth of domestic misery often brought on by untreated menopause, ministers, priests, and rabbis are often more receptive to the idea of hormone therapy than the more traditional-minded members of my own profession.[7]

Feminine Forever is mentioned in most discussions about the history of estrogen therapy. It was considered the benchmark publication that had menopausal women in the '60s beating a path to their doctor's office to get a prescription for the wonder cure for vanishing femininity.

Trouble in Paradise: ERT Is Linked to Endometrial Cancer

Wilson's claims that ERT worked may have proved satisfactory, but his claims of ERT being safe came crashing down in the late '70s with the reported rise of endometrial cancer among women taking estrogen. Endometrial cancer is cancer of the lining of the uterine cavity, commonly called uterine cancer.

Amanda Spake said in the article "The Raging Hormone Debate":

> A decade later, after thousands of women were using the drugs, the bad news started to

65

trickle in: Women on estrogen had eight
times the risk of uterine cancer and might
have increased their risk of breast cancer as
well. Suddenly, the glory days of estrogen
appeared to be over.[8]

The conclusive evidence against ERT came on February 1,
1979, when *The New England Journal of Medicine*
published a shocking report entitled, "Replacement
Estrogens and Endometrial Cancer." It was the definitive
medical data used to substantiate the link between
endometrial cancer and estrogen. The results were
summarized as follows:

> The present study confirms that long-term
> replacement estrogen treatment is strongly
> associated with endometrial cancer.
> Furthermore, in these data, discontinuation of
> estrogen intake is associated with a striking
> decrease in risk of endometrial cancer within
> six months. Whereas the annual risk in non-
> users is about one per thousand, the annual
> risk among all current users is very high—of
> the order of 20 per thousand. Among long-
> term users, the risk is even higher.[9]

Correcting the Dominant Problem: The Evolution to HRT

Since estrogen replacement therapy was meant to
mimic a woman's natural cycle, doctors considered
introducing progesterone into this therapy. Progesterone is
the hormone that causes the sloughing off of the lining of
the uterus. Though women on ERT had replaced the
estrogen in their bodies, they had not replaced

progesterone. Therefore, they were not experiencing the necessary sloughing off of the lining of the uterus. This was at times leading to endometrial hyperplasia. Hyperplasia advances in stages and can eventually lead to cancer.

This discovery prompted the medical community to add progesterone. The added hormone caused women to, once again, slough off the uterine lining as they had with their pre-menopause monthly cycles. This change was believed to protect the endometrium from developing cancer. At this point, the treatment and terminology shifted from ERT to hormone replacement therapy (HRT).

> *Hope is a*
> *waking dream.*
> *—Aristotle*

Early Suspicions: Breast Cancer and HRT

The addition of progesterone to estrogen seemed to solve one problem that occurred in the history of HRT. But then another question was raised: *Is HRT related to the development of breast cancer?*

The opinions of doctors varied on the subject of breast cancer, and this was before the startling results of the Women's Health Initiative. Fortunately the medical community agreed on this one premise—the careful monitoring of women on HRT. In *Managing Your Menopause,* Utian and Jacobowitz explained:

> The most recent study on breast cancer risk appeared in *The New England Journal of Medicine* on August 3, 1989. In it, the risk

appeared to be increased to 1.7 times that for
the general population—still not a dramatic
increase. Yet, it does suggest an increase in risk
rather than confirming our thinking that the
combination of estrogen and progestin would
decrease the risk of breast cancer…. The data
are not conclusive enough to warrant any
immediate change in the way we [doctors]
approach hormone replacement, but they do
show the need for additional research.[10]

The debate about the risk of breast cancer went on for
years, and now we have the results from July 2002 that
confirm an increased risk.

Other Benefits Were Touted

The two most noted reasons in support of HRT use
were the prevention of osteoporosis and prevention of
heart disease.

Osteoporosis is a condition of weakened or brittle
bones that can break easily. It is most often seen in
women after menopause, and the condition is serious. For
example, one woman said that her mother had to have
her backbone replaced with the backbone of a sheep—
before age 40. Another woman said that while she was in
her forties, she had been tested for bone density and was
told she had serious bone deterioration.

There was also a great deal of talk in the medical
community about the positive effects of HRT in the prevention of heart disease or coronary artery disease (CAD).

Again, we now have results from the Women's Health
Initiative that show increased risk for heart disease instead
of increased protection.

We Don't Know What We Don't Know

With the wide variance in medical opinions, it is evident that much is undetermined regarding the safety of treating menopause symptoms. Therefore, we must take responsibility to weigh the options and information that we do have and choose wisely. We know better than to take one person's opinion as gospel truth. With that, even a doctor will agree.

Dr. Lisa Sanders, in her article entitled "Medicine's Progress, One Setback at a Time," said, "The history of medicine is a long, serpentine narrative of the death of old ideas giving way to the birth of new ones. And this cycle is moving faster than ever."[11]

Dr. Sanders recalls the dean of her medical school on the first day telling her and her hopeful classmates, "Half of what we teach you here is wrong—unfortunately, we don't know which half."

Until that time comes, understanding how medical opinions were formed in the past should help us make our own decisions in the future.

What We Can Learn from Our Predecessors

The history of HRT is an illustration—albeit a sad one—of what has happened to women who were exposed to just one side of the issue. They responded to dramatic, yet untested, claims of estrogen as a miracle cure. They took the estrogen to relieve symptoms, and indeed relief came—along with the increased cases of uterine cancer. That problem was corrected, but then another concern arose: Does HRT contribute to breast cancer?

The evidence at that time was inconclusive, so prescriptions were written. However, studies now show that the suspicions about HRT and breast cancer were justified. So, the new question is, What *new* cure for menopausal symptoms will come? And what risks may it bring?

What Does This Mean for You?

When I first wrote this book, I said that we stood at a crossroad. Now it feels more like we are on a moving vehicle—one likely to change course at a moment's notice. Today's news is tomorrow's history.

To better prepare us to live and choose in this uncertainty, we'll walk through the process for making informed decisions in the following chapter.

In his great mercy he has given us new birth into a living hope through the resurrection of Jesus Christ from the dead …
—*1 Peter 1:3b NIV*

A Word of Encouragement

We live in an exciting time. Discoveries abound, and while we may be confused by medical reports and frequent updates, the new information can invoke a more thoughtful decision-making process. This process should include discerning spiritual wisdom as we sort out the pros and cons.

Indeed, human wisdom can help us; but God, through His Son and Holy Spirit, can lift us up in the midst of troubling health issues and walk with us through them. Furthermore, He *is* the Great Physician. Ask Him for insight in choosing the best option for you.

CHAPTER 5

The Process for Making Informed Decisions

Perhaps you are in the very early stages of menopause. You've had a few hot flashes and your memory isn't quite what it used to be. Though you haven't weighed your treatment options yet, you anticipate more distressing symptoms in the future.

If you're further along in this life stage, you may have missed a few periods. Perhaps your doctor has confirmed that you are indeed in menopause. Perhaps he has suggested hormone treatment, so you are in the process of deciding what to do next.

Then again, you may have been on HRT for a number of years. Now you face medical information that contradicts former medical options.

Whatever your situation, you'll likely consider treatment to relieve the symptoms, and you'll have a number of decisions to make: Stay on HRT or get off? Call the doctor today? Believe the new information? Ease the symptoms with HRT? Trust your own doctor's advice?

You may be overwhelmed, given the rate that new information rolls off the presses and the wide variance in professional opinions. Do you wonder, *How do I decide?*

Take heart! I think you'll find relief as you follow the suggestions in the Process for Making Informed Decisions section. You'll also gain confidence as you make wise choices about your health.

To simplify the process for you, I've included a worksheet at the end of this chapter. It summarizes the steps and provides places for you to note your responses. You are free to make multiple copies for your personal use; in fact, I urge you to do so as you start the process. The changing nature of menopause may necessitate that you reevaluate your situation quarterly or yearly. Having a fresh worksheet ready will help get you on your way.

Now, let's get started.

Step 1: Recognize the Need to Reevaluate

While reevaluation seems to be an odd place to start a process, consider how during menopause your body is constantly changing. This state of flux mandates that you adapt—*continually.* The need to reevaluate ends when your body is no longer adapting to the decrease in estrogen.

There are several other reasons your treatment (or non-treatment) options will need a revisit throughout menopause.

1. Menopause is a process that can span ten years or longer; and because of the continual changes, your body may at some point no longer respond favorably to a treatment that has worked for you in the past.

2. Medical opinions fluctuate, causing recommendations to swing from one form of advice to another.

3. If you are on HRT, you may want to consider switching to treatment that has no adverse health risks.

4. If you've not yet considered treatment, the time may come when symptoms demand a pro-active response.

If you're among this last group of women who have not yet decided what to do, perhaps you've actually chosen not to choose. In truth, you may have "chosen" to …

- ride with whatever appears right at the time and hope for the best.

- take your doctor's suggestion without further investigation.

- do what your best friend is doing.

- do what your mother did—if you even
  know what she did.

I know women who take paths of non-action. Recently I ran into a friend I'd not seen for a few years. She asked what I was doing, which led to a discussion about menopause. I asked her if she took hormones. She said she didn't and had never spoken to anyone about the subject. After her last child was born, over twenty years ago, she stopped going to a doctor.

"If anything is wrong," she smiled, "I don't want to know about it."

She chose to ride with whatever happens and hope for the best. This is okay—as long as she does not develop health problems, especially ones that are slow to manifest or are hard to detect.

Check your own attitude. Do you take the path of least resistance when it comes to health-related decisions? Do you rely on your doctor or other people to decide for you?

Beware that each of us tends to pursue a path of least resistance. If you find that you've quieted the night sweats with HRT without having weighed the risks, you may be on that path. Or if you've avoided the OB/GYN, hoping that "ignorance is bliss," your bliss may be short-lived.

Step 2: Evaluate Your Level of Discomfort

With the exception of that one alarming hot flash in the elegant Chicago restaurant, I endured no other embarrassing moments and few sleepless nights. I was uncomfortable but not distressed.

However, your symptoms may demand greater attention or treatment. One of my friends told me she didn't know how she could make it without HRT because her hot flashes disrupted her life. Another friend said, "I still get hot flashes, but I've decided to just live with them."

Everyone is different. Even if your menopause symptoms are similar to those of women you know, you may tolerate them in a completely different way.

In the same way your toleration of symptoms may vary from other women's, your perception of symptoms will vary over time and in recollection. In the worksheet at the end of the chapter, I've included a chart that helps you to qualify each of your symptoms, ranking them 1 through 6. But to prevent evaluations from being swayed by, say, a drenching hot flash, I suggest that you also

> *The wish for healing has ever been the half of health.*
> —*Seneca*

journal your experiences. Describe what you felt or thought at the time. In re-reading your entries later, you may remember the experience more clearly and realize that symptoms are not decreasing; rather, you are more used to them. Or you may discover that things are worse, and it's time to try a different treatment.

This is why adequate treatment includes your decisions and experiences. To benefit from these personal insights, list your symptoms, evaluate their troublesomeness, and include any medications or supplements you currently take.

Step 3: Start a File for Incoming Medical Updates

Organization is key when basing decisions on changing data. I find that the easiest way to track the changes in menopause research is to label one folder, clip the articles, and store them there until I make time to read them.

I find this handy as new information arrives—usually at the most inconvenient times. For example, I clip articles from the *New York Times*. While I may not read them when the paper arrives first thing in the morning, I do have a place to store the updated data whenever it appears in print.

I also recommend keeping a folder on your computer, too. As Web links change and morph, you may encounter less frustration by saving the Web page to a file or by copying the report to a separate document. If you save a link, you may click on it later only to find that the article or site is no longer available.

Step 4: Survey the Current Data

Now that you have your file established, take a bit of time to survey the current data. Your first instinct may be to head to the library or bookstore, but keep in mind that anything written before July 2002 will not have the findings from the Women's Health Initiative reports. You may do well to choose from several periodicals and check them quarterly. Or check the Web sites for medical journals, health organizations, or major newspapers. You can also use the Library of Congress search function to build a list of articles to cross-reference at your local library. Your librarian can help you find them in the periodicals collection and point you to a nearby copy machine. That Web address is http://catalog.loc.gov/.

As you read these articles, keep a highlighter and pen handy— you don't want to have to read these again (at least not closely). Make note of information that seems particularly relevant to someone with your genetic heritage and risk factors. You may discover that you need more specific information on a particular sub-topic. For this, Web searches will help; also check the Web sites listed in Step 9: Investigate Specialized Resources.

Step 5: Weigh the Issues and Rate Your Quality of Life

For decades women have been taking HRT for beneficial quality of life. This rather ambiguous phrase most often relates to the impact of mood swings, memory loss, sleep disturbances, general malaise, and other symptoms.

The results of the federal study

Hormone Replacement Pros and Cons

PROS:

Relieves hot flashes and night sweats.

Reduces vaginal dryness.

Long-term use helps maintain strong bones, although HRT must be then taken for a lifetime.

CONS:

Slightly increases risk of leg blood clots, breast cancer, heart attack and stroke.

Does not help urinary incontinence.

STILL UNKNOWN:

Memory loss/Alzheimer's disease: Studies are ongoing, but no proof exists yet that HRT retards progression of memory loss or Alzheimer's disease.

DEPRESSION:

No convincing evidence that HRT helps major depression.[1]

reported on March 18, 2003 (see page 61), concluding that women on HRT did not experience the benefits of improved quality of life surprised a number of doctors. Dr. Jennifer Hays said:

> We were surprised because of all the anecdotal and clinical reports that women feel better while they are on hormones. It is everything from "I have less pain" to "I am less depressed" to "I am sleeping better" or "I have more energy."[2]

Pharmacist Chris Strong was also surprised at the results of the study, saying:

> I have a lot of names that would not agree with that report. They would be on hormones for the quality of life benefit. I speak with women who are actually debilitated when not on hormones. I find it a strictly personal life decision to what is an acceptable risk as to basic goals of life, and a person should have the freedom to make that decision.[3]

Evaluation of your quality of life is completely subjective. Only you know how well or unwell you feel. Review your symptom ratings from Step 2 and determine if it's time to try a different treatment.

If you decide it's time to try something else, be sure to read about the options in chapter 6. Whatever course you choose, it will be helpful to routinely evaluate how you feel overall—physically, emotionally, and spiritually. Then address specific issues, such as hot flashes, with your doctor and other sources.

Step 6: Talk with Other Women and Note Your Internal Responses

Other women are a great source of information and encouragement. Each one will have a unique journey to share with you; some of the stories will resonate with your own.

Some women, having experienced some of the same frustrations, will understand why you're asking and will be especially willing to talk. Other women will not have experienced many symptoms but are curious (more likely, anxious) about what lies ahead. All will benefit by coming together to share their stories and questions. Consider inviting several friends between the ages of 40 and 55 to join you for a group discussion about menopause.

Several of the groups I interviewed in research for this book enjoyed the fellowship so much that they formed their own support groups. I've included suggestions for forming a support group in the appendix of this book.

As you talk with other women, make note of your internal responses. Are you hesitant about this or that? Information will vary, and you will need to bring your own set of circumstances and health distinctives to bear on that information. One woman may suffer greatly from hot flashes and find no relief aside from HRT. You, on the other hand, may be experiencing minimal discomfort with hot flashes and choose to live through them without medication.

In my own case, I recognized early on that I felt intuitively uncomfortable with the idea of taking HRT. I am adopted, so I don't know my hereditary risks. I did, however, sense a hesitancy in my spirit when other women strongly suggested taking HRT. These internal concerns are ones that are especially good to bring before God, our Great Physician.

As you question, think, and pray about your treatment decisions, write down your thoughts and feelings. Revisit your notes as you move through the menopause process.

Step 7: Schedule an Appointment with Your Doctor; Go with Questions

As you have become more aware of the concerns surrounding menopause, you probably have more questions now than when you started. It's time to take those specific questions to your doctor and get advice about treatment. He (or she) may be aware of even newer studies that have not been discussed in this book or by your friends.

When you go to your appointment, have questions and blank paper in hand. You'll need space to note his responses. Ask for his opinions on the studies discussed in chapter 4 of this book.

Among the questions you ask, include this one: What would you do yourself? If the doctor is male, I suggest, What would you counsel your wife or mother to do? When I interviewed Dr. Lisa Dunham she said, "I look at the information and decide for myself what I would do for my own family, and that's the way I treat my patients."[4]

As you discuss these issues, know that you are under no obligation to decide while you are still in the doctor's

Here is an overview of my menopause timeline—from the first symptoms to the end.

Date: _____

office. Sometimes it is helpful to take your questions and notes home in order to reflect on all of the information you have gathered.

If you wish to wait to decide on a treatment plan, explain this to your doctor at the time. Clarify your options (and write them down, since your memory, at this point, can be elusive) and inquire about the possibility of phoning your doctor later with your decision. If need be, the nurse can work with you in getting a prescription, finding the needed supplements, or implementing your treatment of choice.

The point of this is, the choice is *yours.*

Step 8: Become Your Own Best Advocate

I've talked with many women who would never question what their doctor suggests. In their minds "doctor's orders" apply to all situations, from split-second decisions during a cardiac arrest to long-term commitments to HRT. If this describes you, think back on medical history—the opinions on HRT keep changing, proving that many unknowns remain.

While the medical researchers and doctors are entitled to their opinions, so are you. Your feelings and input deserve attention. If your doctor dismisses your concerns with a wave of the hand, you may need to be more assertive in asking questions.

If you find that your relationship with your doctor is strained, consider how this will influence your decision-making process. Will you be less inclined to ask further questions? Do you feel you will get clear, straightforward answers? Will your doctor recognize the ambiguities in and conflicts between the research results and personal testimonies?

Your answers to these questions may prompt you to search for a new doctor. Start by asking friends for referrals. Then call that office and book a preliminary consultation. Or ask to have a nurse call you back to answer any questions you might have about the doctor's policies, such as: Will the doctor allow enough time to answer my questions? If there is a routine time set for each appointment, may I schedule more time for this particular one? Is the doctor willing to hear from patients about their feelings on treatment? Will he or she consider my preferences in a suggested treatment plan?

Think in terms of a long-range relationship since menopausal symptoms may last for many years. "One quick visit" is not likely to meet your needs. And your needs will likely span your menopause years.

Step 9: Investigate Specialized Sources

Fortunately, the medical community is not standing still, and therefore, neither can we. Researching specialized sources will help you stay current on the latest data. They also will provide answers to some of the questions that you've raised during your menopause research and experiences. Some of these sources include Web sites, seminars, workshops, and women's clinics. Check your local newspaper for seminar schedules; most papers have a once-a-week community calendar that includes a wide range of seminars and workshops. Visit

Web sites routinely and call your local hospital to inquire about women's clinics in your area that specialize in menopause issues.

Be sure to file all new data in your computer or paper files.

Web Sites

The National Heart, Lung, and Blood Institute Health Information Center

www.nhlbi.nih.gov/whi/

information for consumers and health professionals

(301) 592-8573

The Women's Health Initiative

www.whi.org

National Cancer Institute

http://newscenter.cancer.gov/ (search for "estrogen")

questions and answers from the National Cancer Institute about the Women's Health Initiative study

The North American Menopause Society

www.menopause.org

includes advice on alternatives to hormone therapy

(800) 774-5342 automated consumer request line[5]

Step 10: Involve God

In chapter 12 we'll look at how our spiritual lives impact our journey through menopause.

For now, be aware that this will be a significant step in making wise choices. Acknowledge that God, the Great Physician, knows your situation—medically, emotionally, and spiritually. Ask Him to guide you in choosing the best treatment for your body. Do not, however, *substitute* prayer for investigation; do both. This may be how He chooses to answer your prayer.

Step 11: Decide and Change

You've evaluated, researched, talked, thought, and prayed. Now it's time to act.

It is the characteristic excellence of the strong man that he can bring momentous issues to the fore and make a decision about them. The weak are always forced to decide between alternatives they have not chosen.
—Dietrich Bonhoeffer

So … what do you need to do?

Trust your ability to evaluate your own best course of action, taking into consideration your unique scenario and the information available. Then make a choice. If you choose to take a particular supplement, for instance, and it doesn't help you, revisit this process and try something else.

Step 12: Review This Process Periodically

As you have probably guessed by now, making wise health decisions is an ongoing process. You'll be facing medical issues the rest of your life; repeating this process will help you adapt your treatment to ongoing changes in your body and changes in medical understanding.

A Word of Encouragement

You can do this! You and God are the leading experts on what you need to become the woman He intends. Menopause provides an opportunity to grow stronger spiritually as well as physically. As you grow, it will become easier to rest in the confidence that God has you in the palm of His hand and is helping you every step of the way.

My Process for Making Informed Decisions

1. Recognize my need to reevaluate.
   - After reading about the current changes in the medical information regarding HRT, I do NOT see the need to address this issue right now. (Stop here.)
   - After reading about the current changes in the medical information regarding HRT, I DO see the need for me to become informed and make some personal decisions. (Continue.)

2. Evaluate my level of discomfort. (See chart on page 87.)

3. Start a file for incoming medical updates.
   - Started file ❑ date: _____
   - Updated ❑ date: _____
   - Updated ❑ date: _____

4. Survey the current data.
   - Read current newspaper article on menopause.
     ❑ date: _____
     my response: _____
   - Read current magazine article about menopause.
     ❑ date: _____
     my response: _____
   - Read online article about menopause.
     ❑ date: _____
     my response: _____
   - Check local paper for seminars, workshops. Attend if possible. ❑ date: _____
     my response: _____
   - Ask women for referrals for specialized clinics in the area. Attend if possible. ❑ date: _____
     my response: _____

5. Weigh the issues (especially HRT) and evaluate my quality of life.
   notes: _____
   _____

6. Talk with other women and note my internal responses.
   notes: _____
   _____

7. Schedule an appointment with my doctor; go with questions.
   - _____
   - _____
   - _____

Evaluating My Level of Discomfort

	Treatment to Address My Symptoms (medications/supplements)	Effectiveness Scale: 1-6 1 = mild 6 = severe	Other _____ Scale: 1-6 1 = mild 6 = severe
☐ Hot Flashes/Night Sweats			
☐ Vaginal Dryness			
☐ Anxiety/Mood Swings			
☐ Other _____			
☐ Other _____			

8. Become my own best advocate.
   - My response to what my doctor said is
     _____
   - My comfort-level rating in staying with this doctor is ___ (1 is not comfortable at all; 6 is very comfortable).
   - Based on my comfort level, my decision about keeping this doctor is to: ❑ stay ❑ find another doctor.
        (1) Ask other women for referrals.
        (2) Call about booking an "interview appointment."
        (3) Visit new doctor with questions.
        (4) New questions:
   - _____
   - _____
   - _____

9. Investigate specialized sources. This will help me answer the specific questions that have come up during my investigation. I will record this data in some way (notes, printouts) and add these to my file, as I did in steps 3 and 4.
   - Check local paper for seminars, workshops. Attend if possible. ❑ date: _____
     my response: _____
   - Ask other women for referrals for specialized clinics in the area. Attend if possible. ❑ date: _____
     my response: _____

- Skim Web sites for specific answers to menopause issues that are a concern.
  - ❏ date: _____
  - my response: _____
10. Involve God.
    - Take time with God. Ask Him for guidance.
    - His response is _____
    - My intuition, or spirit, says _____
11. Decide and change. Fill in the following chart.
12. I will review this process periodically.
    - My next review date is: _____

Photocopy at 160% for 8.5" X 11" sheet.

My Decisions for Treatment	Things I Need to Get Started	Date to Implement
1.		
2.		
3.		
4.		
5.		
6.		

My next review date is: _____

Hello from College Pharmacy!
Talking with my pharmacist. He's telling me about
hormones, but since they sound a bit alike (estriol,
estradiol, and estrone), I'm getting a bit confused.
If only my memory were here to help!
Wishing I weren't here—
Lois

CHAPTER 6

Treatment Options

Everyone wants to experience physical, emotional, and spiritual well-being; and obviously, the symptoms of menopause can negatively affect each of these areas of life. This chapter discusses treatment options for menopause symptoms, as well as ways to help prevent some of the health risks associated with aging, such as heart disease and osteoporosis.

Compounding Pharmacies

If you find that your symptoms are more than you can bear, yet you hesitate at the concept of taking HRT, consider the possibility of taking a compounded hormone. This alternative treatment is blended to your doctor's specifications, oftentimes with the intent of lowering the ratio of "harmful" hormones—ones that, in high doses, are thought to contribute to breast cancer and other complications that are associated with conventional HRT use. With this return to ancient pharmacopoeia, the number of "compounding pharmacies"—which may be a new term to you—is increasing in the United States.

As Chris Strong, Doctor of Pharmacy, explained, compounding pharmacies are mostly found in independent pharmacies as compared to chain stores. He said,

> They usually have regular retail products and compound different products that are not available commercially. Compounding pharmacies are really the modern version of original pharmacies. Prescriptions are mixed on the premises to the specifications of physicians for their patients. [Pharmacists] aren't allowed to make compounded formulas that are available by prescription from commercial manufacturers.[1]

Chris is a consultant pharmacist at College Pharmacy in Colorado Springs, Colorado, where female hormone compounds make up 75% of their total compounded prescriptions.

College Pharmacy's most prescribed compound is called *biest,* meaning "two estrogens." This compound was developed years ago by physicians to treat menopause symptoms with less risk than standard HRT prescriptions.

The compound is 80% estriol and 20% estradiol. In his interview, Chris explained how this ratio may be safer:

> Most commercial products are estradiol only. This compound, with less estradiol, is what makes it risk-reducing. Estradiol is the strongest of the three estrogens [in a woman's body], and it has the most tissue-stimulating characteristics. Tissue stimulation can cause cells to proliferate (multiply). If left unchecked, this can lead to tumor growth. We combine estradiol and estriol, and [we] are able to control the same symptoms, using less estradiol than the commercially manufactured products.* The type of product [or "formulation"]—tablet or transdermal gel—is decided by the patient's physician, and we fill it to the physician's specifications.

> The estradiol in prescriptions in the United States—used by commercial manufacturers and by compounding pharmacies—is standardized, approved, and regulated by the FDA. It is recommended to be combined with progesterone, unless a physician doesn't want it.

In a *New York Times* article titled "A User's Guide for Those Who Choose Hormone Replacements," Dr. Michelle P. Warren expresses reservations about compounding pharmacies, "It worries me because they do not have quality control, and with hormones that's really

---

* Commercial estrogen products such as ethinyl estradiol are 1,000 times stronger than estradiol, the strongest estrogen produced by the female body.[2]

very important. I tell patients, if you feel strongly about taking these pharmacy compounds, it will be very difficult for me to determine how much you're taking."[3] In a phone interview with Dr. Warren in May 2003, she explained her specific concerns with products from compounding pharmacies.

"Drug companies have to test their products for [the] exact measurement of estradiol that is in each product. Compounding pharmacies don't have to do that."

Dr. Warren further explained that she has had patients who have had trouble after taking products from compounding pharmacies. Some women had bleeding, and when a blood test was done, [the test revealed that] they had high levels of estradiol in their blood streams. Other women [who were] taking the medication for relief of hot flashes would still have the hot flashes, and their blood tests would show little to no estradiol in their blood streams.

"It's the fluctuating amount of estradiol in the products that I am concerned with," Dr. Warren said. "Because compounding pharmacies don't have to do the testing that the drug companies do, measurements are not always accurate."[4]

In response to Dr. Warren's comments, Chris Strong explained that these discrepancies may result from the varying efficiencies of different types of formulations. (See "Hormones: Ways, Shapes, and Forms" at the end of the chapter.) As a result, those variances can show up in lab tests, even when the dosages are the same. He believes this is more likely the problem than inaccurate measurements being made at the compounding pharmacy. Strong said in a later interview:

> For instance, an oral progesterone will read accurately on a saliva test, but a transdermal (such as a cream applied to the skin) has been shown in studies to produce a false high reading on a saliva test with the same dosage in both cases.
>
> [Dr. Warren] is right in that the performance of products will vary from one compounding pharmacy to another based on what formulations the pharmacy is using. This is why it is important to obtain products from a pharmacy that specializes in the particular formulations being prescribed and that the pharmacist is able to offer guidance to the physician based on his knowledge of the product. I would have to say that all the physicians that work with us on hormone replacement are pleased with their patient outcomes.[5]

Given this controversy, it would be good to talk with your own doctor about the use of compounded treatment and the reliability of compounding pharmacies in your area.

Two Medical Opinions About Treatment for Symptoms

Lisa Dunham, M.D.

Many of my menopausal patients respond well to HRT for hot flashes. However, leaving someone on HRT for life is not necessary because hot flashes eventually go away. I still allow women to use it for two to three years and then I ask them to start tapering off. Both soy supplements and black cohosh are available over the counter for relief of menopausal symptoms. I also have a few patients reporting some success with vitamin E. Unfortunately there are no studies available assessing long-term safety.

> *Leaving someone on HRT for life is not necessary because hot flashes eventually go away.*
> *—Dr. Lisa Dunham*

Doctors also prescribe anti-depressants for mood swings and some [women] see improvement.

In making a decision I would suggest:

1. Try going naturally first.

2. Try the over-the-counter preparation, Estroven. It has soy and black cohash.

3. If you're still not doing well, either try an anti-depressant or go on hormones.

4. After a couple of years try to wean back and see how you do.

5. Use the most common sense approach.[6]

Dr. Dunham is with the Mountain View Medical Group in Colorado Springs, Colorado.

Regarding my health, here are some things I wish I'd done—or had not done—earlier in my life.

Also, here are some things I'm glad that I have done for my health …

Date: _____

Bruce Kahn, M.D.

In a telephone interview with Dr. Kahn, I asked him to respond to the results of the WHI study reported in the July 10, 2002, *New York Times* article.

> If you look at the data, the average age of women when they entered the study was 63. This does not reflect the population starting HRT in the perimenopausal age.
>
> There was an increase in the risk of heart attack, stroke, and blood clots in the group of women being studied, but they also found that there was good protection for hip fracture and colon cancer. When you look at the data, it looks like a bad risk, but when you look at it over the whole six years of the study, there were 30 cases of heart disease among 10,000 women taking the placebo and 37 cases of heart disease among 10,000 women taking HRT.[7]

Dr. Kahn went on to say that the important thing to remember is that medical findings, like any news, can be expressed from varying perspectives. He felt that the newspaper coverage on this study was being sold to the public with the emphasis placed on risk factors and that the risk factors were made to sound worse than they really are.

He also expressed concern that this information was released to the media before it was given to physicians. This raised some suspicions in his mind as to the ulterior motives of the people doing the study.

Another study was released to the media before physicians were informed. That article opened with this statement:

> Confounding a widely held impression, a large federal study has found that hormone therapy for menopause does not affect quality of life.[8]

Dr. Kahn was again surprised that this coverage made headline news without physicians having been alerted first.

Dr. Kahn also told me that he has a bias on this issue since he is involved in a study that is supported by Wyeth Pharmaceutical Company, the manufacturers of Prempro—a hormone therapy. The current work involves the development of the next generation of HRT.

When patients come into Dr. Kahn's office seeking relief from menopausal symptoms, he carefully takes them through a number of charts that explain the results of the WHI study. His intent is to give his patients the information in the context of hard figures.

> The WHI study only stopped one arm of the study: women on a combination of estrogen and progestin. The study continues for women on estrogen alone.
>
> When women come to me for relief from menopausal symptoms, there is nothing like estrogen. Nothing like estrogen.
>
> So has this study changed the ways I am going to prescribe HRT? Yes. I am going to be much less likely to start a woman in her sixties on HRT. But the bulk of the women I

see are between the ages of 47 and 53. I do agree with the findings of the study that HRT should not be prescribed for protection against heart disease. It does offer excellent protection for osteoporosis.

A woman who is 50 and starts HRT and stays on it for five years, goes off it and still has symptoms ... can go back on it.[9]

Dr. Kahn further stated that there is a risk for an increase in breast cancer but that there is no data that shows an increased risk of *dying* from breast cancer, "Either the breast cancer that women get is being diagnosed early and treated better, or the cancer they get on HRT is less aggressive and treated better."

Dr. Kahn works in the Department of Obstetrics and Gynecology of the Scripps Clinic in La Jolla, California.

As you can see, even professionals have varying opinions about what to prescribe for their patients. This is all the more reason for women to work through the Process for Making Informed Decisions worksheet and determine which treatments suit them best.

Treatment for Hot Flashes

I did not experience many hot flashes, and all were milder than my first one in that Chicago restaurant. After starting to take vitamin E (800 IU a day), the hot flashes disappeared altogether. Whenever I went off vitamin E, they started again. After about a year, I reduced the dosage to 400 IU a day and was fine.

This treatment may work for you as well, but before taking vitamin E, check with your doctor about the right dosage, especially if you have liver disease. Also inquire about potential interactions with any other medications you are taking. You may need to switch to alternate medications in some cases. Your doctor can help you make the wisest choice.

In a *Parade* magazine article, Dr. Isadore Rosenfeld recommends asking your doctor about taking an antidepressant such as Prozac or Effexor for hot flashes and/or mood swings.[10]

Treatment for Mood Swings

This is probably the most distressing symptom of menopause previously thought relieved by HRT. The results of a study reported in the *New York Times* article of March 18, 2003, casts real doubt on the actual effectiveness of HRT for this quality-of-life issue.

However, one woman participating in one of my focus groups has returned to HRT. When she was not using hormones, she was hospitalized for depression and anxiety. She reports that her symptoms are alleviated by HRT. For her, the risks do not outweigh the benefits.

The study results did not impress another woman I spoke with recently. She has had breast cancer, yet she has chosen to return to HRT because she is certain it greatly increases her sense of well-being.

Women seeking relief from emotional fluctuations due to menopause will have to evaluate the intensity and severity of these symptoms. For mood swings, depression, anxiety, or a general sense of malaise, doctors are now experimenting with the effectiveness of antidepressants. These have helped some women who refuse HRT but need treatment for their mood-related symptoms.

As women evaluate their emotional symptoms, they should keep in mind that some of the stresses of mid-life are not related to menopause, and these stresses may contribute to emotional imbalance. Around this time of life, women face many challenges: children grow up and leave home; aging parents decline in health; and finances change as one approaches retirement age. Furthermore, since the dawning of this post-September 11 era, many men and women of all ages have expressed to me that they have feelings of anxiety for no personal reason. Certainly the threats of this era (including terrorism, war, and financial instability) affect our sense of well-being. All of these factors should be considered in evaluating which moods are symptomatic or circumstantial.

> *Doctors are now experimenting with the effectiveness of antidepressants. These have helped some women who refuse HRT but need treatment for their mood-related symptoms.*

Fortunately, two circumstantial factors weigh in favorably. The first—God's involvement—is constant and promised (Isaiah 43:2). The second, relaxation, is one that menopausal women should gladly adopt. These are discussed in chapter 12 and chapter 8, respectively.

Treatment for Vaginal Dryness and Diminished Libido

Vaginal dryness and diminished libido are particularly frustrating side-effects of menopause. Dr. Isadore Rosenfeld recommends that you ask your doctor about three possible remedies: testosterone supplements to increase libido, topical lubricants for vaginal dryness, and topical estrogen. With topical estrogen, only "very small amounts of the hormone are absorbed into the blood stream."[11]

College Pharmacy carries a product called "Crème de la Femme" which I have found helpful with vaginal dryness. It includes an applicator for internal use, which many other lubricants do not include.

A decrease in libido can be a difficult symptom to treat, and it can result from more than just hormone changes. Talk with your doctor and your husband. Keep in mind that when the natural sex drive is diminished, hidden relationship problems can surface. This result may provide inroads for discussion on topics that couples, at this more mature life stage, may now be more willing to talk about. It is important to realize that you can enjoy a healthy sex life well past menopause, but it will be based more on a caring and loving relationship than on hormonal desire. Communication is one of the best ways to address this issue.

Prevention and Treatment for Osteoporosis

You may have seen the ads about symptoms of osteoporosis—there are none, save a broken bone. I noticed that the ads included the risk factors, and since I had none (that I knew of for certain), I ignored the warnings about this bone-thinning disease. Of the factors in the list below, I did not have to worry about the first five. With the last one—a family history of osteoporosis —I couldn't be sure. As I am adopted, I don't know my birth family's health history. Here are the red flags:

smoking cigarettes

being very thin

having an eating disorder, such as anorexia

having fewer than normal menstrual periods

using medications such as corticosteroids or anticonvulsants

a family history of osteoporosis[12]

All of these factors should be self-evident, but the conclusive evidence is not. Fortunately, a bone-density scan can diagnose this disease; the test is simple and quick. My doctor urged me to take one; I agreed. There was no need to fast or follow any preliminary regimen. I simply lay on a table and the machine traveled above me, scanning up and down my body. I received the results in minutes.

That's when I was completely shocked. I was diagnosed with osteopinia, a condition of significant bone thinning. It is not quite as severe as osteoporosis, but I was told it should be taken seriously.

I learned of my condition just before the closing of my opportunity window to prevent osteoporosis, and I have faithfully followed my doctor's recommendations for prevention. While I had taken calcium tablets only sporadically before, I now take 600 mg of calcium (coupled with 200 IU of vitamin D) each and every day. I walk for thirty minutes, four or five days a week, and I work out with weights three days a week.

The sooner a woman starts a similar regimen, the greater her chances of preventing osteoporosis. If she is over 50 and has not had a bone-density scan, she should talk with her doctor about scheduling one. At this time, she may also inquire about the new medications that help improve bone density levels. These include Fosamax, Miacalcin, and Evista.[13]

> *"When you pass through the waters, I will be with you; And through the rivers, they shall not overflow you. When you walk through the fire, you shall not be burned, Nor shall the flame scorch you."*
> —Isaiah 43:2

Prevention of Heart Disease

To prevent heart disease, start with diagnostic testing. Schedule a cholesterol reading through your doctor's office, and have your blood pressure checked regularly. High readings in these two variables may indicate impending heart disease.

If your blood test indicates high cholesterol, your doctor will suggest specific changes in your diet or, perhaps, drugs that help to lower cholesterol. It is important to continue to be monitored with follow-up blood tests and doctor visits.

The next chapter outlines diet and exercise and their relation to overall health. These disciplines are especially helpful in preventing heart disease, but they also have tremendous impact in self-confidence, emotions, and bone strength. While there are differing opinions as to which diet and what exercises are best, it seems that professionals agree on some general guidelines that can improve women's health.

A Word of Encouragement

So much has been discovered since our mothers and grandmothers went through menopause. We are blessed to have help that they did not. We can rejoice, too, that God remains involved in every aspect of our lives. He is weaving new threads of His grace through our very being all the time.

Hormones: Ways, Shapes, and Forms

There is so much information involving hormone therapy, it's easy to become confused. The following may help you better evaluate your treatment options.

Compounded Formulations: Different Ways, Shapes, and Forms

The various formulations that are compounded to treat menopause symptoms include the following:

capsule or tablet: ingested orally and processed through the liver. This digestion causes an initial breakdown of the hormone before it reaches the bloodstream and therefore makes it less effective.

topical gel or cream: applied directly to the skin inside the wrists, on the abdomen, or behind the knees and immediately absorbed into the bloodstream. Immediate absorption brings faster and more reliable results.

lozenge: dissolved orally and absorbed directly into the bloodstream. Lozenges or topical formulations remain the preferred methods of treatment for two reasons: They absorb readily and they avoid passing through the liver directly.

vaginal cream: inserted vaginally and absorbed directly into the bloodstream. Although absorption is immediate, the method is less convenient than the other three formulations.

Hormones: All-Natural, Bio-identical, or Synthetic?

Hormone therapy formulations are based on estradiol—one of the three hormones that occur naturally in a woman's body. The natural balance of human estrogens is 60%-80% estriol, 10%-20% estradiol, and 10%-20% estrone. Hormone formulations are either synthetically or naturally based.

Synthetic hormone formulations are made using chemically altered estradiol. This alteration increases the potency of the synthetic product so that it is stronger than what occurs naturally in the female body. Most manufactured HRTs are synthetic, including tablets such as Ogen, Estratab, and Femhrt.

Some naturally based HRTs are manufactured. One exception to the synthetic verses natural categorization is Premarin. This HRT tablet is made from hormones taken from the urine of pregnant mares. While the hormone is indeed natural, it is *not* natural to a woman's body.

Strictly speaking, a *natural hormone* comes directly from a plant source. A purely natural hormone, such as yam or black cohosh, can be purchased in tablet form at health food stores.

Natural hormones that are compounded for pharmaceutical use are called *bio-identical hormones*. These compounded products include natural hormones (from wild yam or soy) and are formulated in a FDA-certified lab to be physiologically identical to human hormones. This match causes them to function in the same way as the body's own hormones. In the U.S., compounding pharmacies use natural hormones in HRT formulations (no synthetics). The estrogen ratios in bio-identical hormones are specified according to ratios in the typical female body. Since the ratio of estradiol is lower than in synthetic HRT formulations, compounded formulations are not as strong and are therefore considered risk-reducing when compared to conventional HRT.[14]

Hello!
Dashing off to my exercise club. It's just a mile away, but ... I think I'll drive there and back.
Hey, at least I'm going!
Wishing I weren't here—

Lois

CHAPTER 7

Preventative Measures: Diet and Exercise

I know what you're thinking. You want to skip this chapter because you already know what will be written about diet and exercise, and it will not be fun. I agree. Oh, that we could eat what we want and lie around, and all would be well!

Were that possible, my indulgence of choice would be fats. One of my favorite treats is to put butter (real butter, not any low-fat variety of almost-butter) on chocolate cake. Yes, I said cake. My father taught me this little-known delicacy and, let me tell you, it is wonderful!

And, of course, corn on the cob is a traditionally excellent vehicle for more butter. When I was growing up, we lived about two hours south of New York City. In the summer, my family would go to Coney Island to spend a day riding the Steeplechase and roller coaster. My father and I would pause between rides for a drenched-in-a-vat-of-butter ear of corn.

My mother, on the other hand, often declined the indulgence because she was not blessed with the galloping metabolism my father and I enjoyed. I remember many times joining my father for a late-night bacon, lettuce, and tomato sandwich. No nightmares or sleepless nights because of overworked digestive systems for us!

What I don't remember from that era is one word of caution about too much fat, and I remember only a few words about rationing sweets. Not that any words from the experts would have mattered to my father. He was the consummate food lover. And since he didn't like to dine alone, I was his cohort in high-fat consumption.

Neither my father nor I were ever overweight. My mother would gain weight just smelling food. The apparent difference was the high metabolic rate my father and I enjoyed and the low metabolic rate my mother endured. That seemed decidedly unfair.

Menopausal Metabolism

Now, however, I am sadly aware that my metabolic processes no longer burn with the speed of a furnace but rather at the pace of dying embers. By mid-life, those of us who have escaped weight problems join the masses in the battle of the bulge.

I am sadly aware that my metabolic processes no longer burn with the speed of a furnace but rather at the pace of dying embers.

So whether or not you have experienced the diet roller coaster; at menopause, you will likely need to face the diet monster. I promise not to bore you with suggested meal plans or rules for counting calories, fat grams, or carbohydrates. But heed the warning you already know: being overweight, especially as you age, can severely damage your health.

Nothing I can say here will change your eating habits if you are not convinced it is worth the Herculean effort. Overcoming unhealthy eating habits is not easy, but the benefits are worth pursuing. This wasn't easy for me— it's *still* not easy for me—but speaking from experience, I can assure you that you truly will feel better physically and emotionally.

A Healthy Attitude Shift

In chapter 3, I mentioned the notorious ten pounds that usually arrive with menopause. I still have not been able to shed them. I tried crash diets to no avail. Then I finally accepted the fact that I will never again weigh what I weighed most of my adult life.

This is not all bad news. Because I had been relatively thin most of my life, I could afford to gain ten pounds and not be overweight. The acceptance of my current weight has more to do with a change of attitude about what is attractive. After a lifetime of aiming at thin, I finally started to let go of the fantasy that lingerie models are the norm for all womanhood (not that I ever did have a shape anything like those sculpted forms).

> *Those who think they have not time for bodily exercise will sooner or later have to find time for illness.*
> —*Edward Stanley, Earl of Derby*

Furthermore, being thin is not necessarily equivalent to being healthy. We can be so consumed with pursuing a wispy look that we can deny our bodies healthy nutrition. My current weight is well within healthy guidelines for a woman of my age and frame. It is no longer thin, but it is far from fat.

If you have struggled with dieting and weight loss for a long time, consider your motivation. Is it appearance or health? While the first is valid, it may not seem important enough when you're choosing between cheesecake or fruit parfait. Of the women I interviewed, those who claimed that they needed to lose weight admitted that the determining factor was appearance, not health. Consider an attitude shift. Would your health prompt you to stay with your plan?

Whatever you weigh as you enter menopause, realize that your metabolism will change—if it hasn't already. If you continue to eat what you always have, you will gain weight. If you cut down, you will lose or maintain weight.

This is what I know about my mother's menopause experience ...
(I will also note anything I happen to know about your paternal grandmother's experience.)

Date: _____

More Than One Opinion

The methods of "cutting down" vary widely. In my case, my cholesterol was a little high, so my doctor recommended a low-fat diet with moderate carbohydrate consumption. She suggested that I keep bread products (my carb of choice) to no more than three or four a day. Now that *is* reasonable. I can have a piece of toast at breakfast, a sandwich at lunch, and a small serving of rice at dinner.

A good friend of mine recently went on a high-fat, high-protein, low-carb diet. She felt great; her energy level increased, and she lost a lot of weight.

While the term *high-fat diet* may surprise you, some reports now say that this type of diet is not the risk factor for heart disease it was once believed to be. A recent report in *The New England Journal of Medicine* suggests that this diet may actually increase the levels of HDL (or good) cholesterol and triglycerides in the body, though it does not seem to change the LDL (or bad) cholesterol levels or blood pressure readings.[1]

This seemed like good news, and since I had hoped to lose a little weight, I too went on the high-fat diet. I lasted three days! Depriving myself of my "mainstay" foods made the low-carb diet a huge challenge. I know that *challenge* is the operative word in any diet regimen, but the moderate, low-fat diet that my doctor recommended was less challenging for me, and therefore, I am able to stay on it longer.

My point here is that we are all different. What my doctor recommends for me may not be at all what you should do.

The Honest Struggle

I will be honest and admit that developing healthy eating habits in my fifties is an ongoing challenge. When I indulge, telling myself, *I can; I'm not overweight,* I ignore my own advice about choosing my diet according to what's healthy. Whether it goes to my hips is not the issue. The real issue is how that food affects my entire system.

My cholesterol level testifies to that. It used to be that I could eat anything I wanted. I wouldn't gain a pound or raise my cholesterol a bit. But those days are gone.

Admitting the struggle is part of the solution to healthy eating. Our bodies change during and after menopause. Even those of us foolish enough to think it would never happen to us need to face reality.

So, *be honest with yourself.*

As you do, you can approach the matter of changing your eating habits by using the Process for Informed Decisions worksheet at the end of chapter 5. Consider the many suggestions for healthy weight and diet, and consult your doctor on these issues, too.

My investigation into these matters has been an eye-opener. On the way out the door to go to a movie with a girlfriend, my husband, Steve, stopped me with a newspaper clipping. It said that movie theater popcorn with "butter" has 1,640 calories and 126 grams of fat!

Food Facts

Cheese fries with ranch dressing
    3010 calories, 217 grams of fat

Movie theatre popcorn with "butter" topping (large)
    1640 calories, 126 grams of fat

Fettuccini Alfredo
    1500 calories, 97 grams of fat

Beef and cheese nachos with sour cream and guacamole
    1360 calories, 89 grams of fat

Denny's meat-lover's skillet
    1150 calories, 93 grams of fat

Subway's subs with 6 grams of fat or less
    about 260 calories, 5 grams of fat

McDonald's fruit and yogurt parfait
    380 calories, 5 grams of fat

Pasta with red clam or marinara sauce
    870 calories, 24 grams of fat

Fajitas with tortillas
    840 calories, 24 grams of fat[2]

I would have loved to ignore that information and simply enjoyed my bucket of popcorn. But, wow!—that would have to be pretty good popcorn to justify the fat intake. Of course, it's okay to splurge once in a while, but I use information like this to gauge just how often I do.

Get Moving

We were touring in Ireland a few years ago and spent the night at a quaint bed and breakfast in the seaside town of Kinsale. Our hostess was a lovely woman in her fifties, fit and trim and talkative.

While eating breakfast I asked her if she worked out.

"You mean in a club darlin'?" she said in her congenial Irish brogue.

"Well, yes."

She went on to tell me that the Irish don't have need of such clubs because they walk a lot every day. (Though I would venture to say that larger Irish cities have them.) And a friend of mine who lived in Amsterdam for several years claimed that she ate whatever she wanted, but she didn't gain a pound during her stay because she walked everywhere.

In contrast, America is a country of motor-riding people. Unlike Europe, most of our towns and cities don't have stores within walking distance of our homes. We couldn't walk to the grocery store and return with packages if we wanted to.

On the other hand, we have become a bit lazy. We want parking places that are close to our destinations, we take escalators instead of stairs, and we gather our stash of remote controls near our easy chairs as we settle in for an evening's entertainment.

I do all of those things. It's ingrained in me to save time and energy by using these devices. However, I recognize that the energy saved in one arena must be burned in another if I am to keep my health as I age.

For this reason, I am committed to exercising. Now, which particular plan, I can't say at the moment. I often get bored with one plan after a few weeks. Then I try something else.

And that's what I suggest for you, too—try something. If you fall off that wagon, hop on another one.

My recent plan of choice is exercising at a club called Curves for Women. Frankly, the only reason I joined is because it is one mile from my house. Other exercise clubs I've joined before have been a 20- to 30-minute drive from home, and I just couldn't keep up the time commitment.

> *And that's what I suggest for you, too—try something. If you fall off that wagon, hop on another one.*

Curves, though, is working out well for me. It takes exactly 30 minutes, and the workout combines weight training with aerobic exercise. I have the accountability of registering how often I go, and I weigh in every month. It is a pleasant atmosphere with encouraging people—all women, and many around my age.

The important thing is to keep looking for something that works for you. My friend who lived in Amsterdam has found that she stays with long walks more than any other kind of exercise. Another friend takes step classes at the YMCA near her home.

You may choose something entirely different. Just don't give up. Get moving.

Finding That Sense of Well-Being

Not everyone can join an exercise club. It can be costly in both time and money. If either applies to you, consider the numerous at-home programs that are available in books or on video or DVD. As you choose from the variety of workout programs, consider the benefits you seek. Weight-bearing exercises help prevent osteoporosis and improve muscle tone. Aerobic exercise strengthens your heart. Since osteoporosis and heart disease are two risks for menopausal women, these two types of exercise are wonderful additions to your health regimen.

This is all easy to say, but please know that exercise is still a discipline for me. It competes for my time against a myriad of other things. I always have to psych myself up before exercising, but I *always* feel better for having done it.

That sense of well-being is not unfounded. Dr. Wulf Utian and Ruth Jacobowitz explain how exercise helps enhance mood and benefit the body physically:

> Exercise offers emotional benefit as well as physical energy by altering your state of mood. This alteration probably occurs because exercise activates the release of certain hormones within the brain that we call the *central endorphins* or *brain morphines*. They produce that special sense of well-being that we experience after exercise.[3]

A Word of Encouragement

All of this mid-life prevention and maintenance may seem daunting, especially at first, but take heart. You will learn, step by step, what works best for you, and you will become familiar with your body in new and wonderful ways.

Hello from my back deck—
It has a view of the eastern slope of the Rockies
that is gorgeous! I've spent a lot of time out here
in the Colorado sunshine, but now, I regret not
having used more sunscreen.
Wishing I weren't here—

Lois

CHAPTER 8

Relaxation Breaks: By Yourself, with Others, with God

It is amazing to me that we, as Americans, can't seem to figure out how to slow down. I don't know anyone who really does a great job of living at a reasonable pace. Young, old, it doesn't matter—we are a driven people. We read books on how to relax; however, we only manage to alter our lifestyles for about two weeks. Most of the women I interviewed were as busy at mid-life as they were when they were thirty. They were doing different things, but they were still moving at the same frantic pace.

Often, the onset of menopause demands an adjustment. Our bodies are changing so dramatically that they can't continue to carry us speeding along in the fast lane like they used to. The time comes to intentionally take relaxation breaks.

The Warmth of the Sun

We live in Colorado, and our house sits on the crest of a hill that is seven thousand feet above sea level. Our back deck is unshaded and overlooks the front range of the Rocky Mountains. Pikes Peak rises above her court of smaller mountains, piercing the crystal blue sky. This is where I like to relax.

It's my idea of perfect—sitting in a lawn chair, basking in the warmth of the sun. This is one of the times I can sit still. It calms me to sit quietly and feel the sun's rays spill over my body, penetrating me with heat.

This is a long-time habit, and unfortunately I didn't use sunscreen until a few years ago. I am afraid I have paid the price. My even tan has been replaced by sun-spotted skin with wrinkles that could have been eliminated by using lotion.

So now I use sunscreen. It definitely slows the tanning process, but it can't take away the sensation of resting in a sun-drenched chaise lounge.

Perhaps your backyard is more rain-soaked than sun-soaked. If so, please don't try to re-create the same experience with a tanning booth. Not only does it damage your

120

skin, it just isn't the same as being out in God's beauty. Wait for summer days (and wear sunscreen!) to indulge in this rejuvenating pastime. It will warm your soul.

A Hot Soak in the Tub

Bubble baths do not require sunshine. They don't require darkness either, though candlelight and evening hours seem appropriate, since that's usually when time allows.

It's also often that by evening time, all of the changes seem to be too much. At that point, escape for a hot soak in the tub. The water will soothe your tired, tense muscles. Add candlelight and classical music, too; they will distract your eyes and ears from everyday stressors.

To prepare your bath, choose from the countless kinds of bubbles, salts, crystals, and oils to add to the water. Candles come in equally numerous scents, sizes, and shapes. Some special bath packages include floating candles to place in the water with you or in a water bowl nearby.

Once in the tub, let your mind relax with your body. Think over the events of the day, or simply let your mind wander. You may find yourself praying. What a peaceful time. Afterward soothe your skin with a rich lotion or cream to prevent dryness.

The Art of Catnapping

I have a friend who used to be an accomplished catnapper. He could work long, productive days because he could nap almost anywhere.

121

One morning he had to take his wife to work before sunrise. Knowing he would be tired later if he didn't nap, he grabbed a pillow from their sofa on his way out the door, planning to catch a few *Z*'s at the office. Once there, he turned out the light, drew the blinds, stretched out on the floor with his pillow, and fell asleep right away. A little later his secretary came into work, right on time. While pacing through his office to reach the light switch, she stumbled over his sleeping body. The dear woman thought he had had a heart attack and almost had one herself.

Though sleeping in the middle of the office floor at pre-dawn hours is not recommended, I do suggest taking short naps to get through long and stressful days.

Because menopause often drains a woman's energy, anything that can add an energy boost is helpful. Short naps—about fifteen minutes—are optimal. One friend of mine lies down on her bed fully dressed every afternoon for just fifteen to twenty minutes. Then, she is up again and ready to go.

A key to truly resting may be to stretch out completely. It is difficult to relax deeply with the head up. Stretching the body out completely will permit total relaxation and provides a refreshing energy boost in the middle of frantic days.

Time with a Friend

Women have been teased for years about spending hours talking on the phone. The teasing has often come from men who spend all of their days on the phone in noisy offices and can't imagine why anyone would choose to spend a moment more with the instrument.

Many women, by the time they reach mid-life, are working outside the home. They probably do not experience the isolation that can occur during child-rearing years, but neither are they finding meaningful interaction with others during the course of a work day.

Calling a friend does not have to take long. It can simply be a moment in the middle of the day when one woman connects with another, providing encouragement for both parties. Sometimes talking to a sympathetic listener about how you feel diffuses the unpredictability that surrounds menopause. While e-mail has its benefits, none seem to fill the need for the voice-to-voice connection that most women need at this season.

> *While e-mail has its benefits, none seem to fill the need for the voice-to-voice connection that most women need at this season.*

One of my dearest friends, Loretta, is a nurse. She and I talk several times a week while we are each fixing dinner. Both of our husbands arrive home late, so we take advantage of a few moments at the end of our days to touch base. Loretta is younger than I am, so she is not experiencing menopause yet. But she is a sensitive listener, and her experience with medical issues gives her an insight that I don't have.

Don't panic if your personal phone directory has no names with *R.N.* behind them. You don't need a medical professional—just a trusted friend to bring life back into perspective. Our lives are often so rushed that we can be isolated in a crowd. We may never find the close relationships where our mothers found them—talking over the backyard fence while hanging laundry. A phone call can replace that loss of intimacy.

> *It is a happy talent to know how to play.* —*Emerson*

Dee, a single mother, summarized the benefits of shared time-outs. "I am so impressed by the sense that, at some level, all of us know how hard it is for women to do all they can do because of how much is demanded of them. [Friends] have been so generous of heart and spirit to help me. It raised in me a great desire to pass on some of that generosity to other women."

Feeding Our Spirits

Blank books are a popular consumer item. Any large bookstore will devote a section to these journals that so artistically encase our intimate thoughts. Some opt for the more practical, inexpensive spiral notebook for journaling. But whatever the cover, journals house our deepest, most precious thoughts.

A friend of mine has been journaling for over ten years and has asked me to promise that when she dies, I will retrieve her journals and dispose of them, unread. She writes her journals in the form of letters to God, and she pours her heart out openly to Him. They are for her alone, and that is the purpose of most journaling— a safe and private way to express our deepest thoughts and feelings.

I don't address my journal entries to God, but I do include prayer lists in my journal. I also jot down two categories of thoughts to help me see how God has moved me from anxiousness to peace: *On my heart* and *Peace.* I ask myself, *What am I worried about?* I write down whatever comes to mind under *On my heart.* Then I think about what feels settled and secure to me and write that down under *Peace.*

As time goes by, I can glance back at these two category entries and see how my anxious feelings have been resolved. Life doesn't always turn out the way I hoped, but I am able to see more clearly how the Lord moved through a situation and changed my anxiety into understanding, action, or acceptance.

When anxiety or mood swings swoop in on you, try journaling to calm yourself and regain focus. Begin by writing freely; don't worry about making sense or being grammatically correct. This will only be seen by you.

The very act of moving thoughts from your mind onto paper releases some tension and allows room for fresh thoughts to come in. You may find that you actually experience new insights about yourself and an awareness of God's gentle voice in the midst of your mental chaos.

Chronicling the Faithfulness of God

A number of years ago, a dramatic example of that process—moving from anxiety to peace—filled the pages of my journal. My son-in-law, Craig, was a junior in college with a promising career in professional baseball well within his grasp. He was a left-handed pitcher who was being recruited by a number of professional teams. The letters and phone calls were pouring in. He and my daughter, Lara, were planning a December wedding. The date was based on Craig being drafted by a team the previous June.

Then Craig started to have terrible pain in his left shoulder. He continued to play, ignoring the pain, until he could no longer deny that something was wrong. They called to tell us that he was going to the doctor. Under *On my heart* I wrote, "Worried about Craig's shoulder."

The next day they called back with the news that the doctor, after looking at X rays, thought Craig might have a cyst or tumor. My heart sank. The word *tumor* made it to the pages of my journal. The days between Craig having an MRI (another form of X ray) taken and the results being given were agony. In fact, during that time I couldn't write anything under *Peace* in my journal.

Craig, gratefully, did not have a tumor. The doctor told him that what he had seen on the X ray turned out to be a bone spur, which had significantly damaged the tendons in his left arm. I was overwhelmed with thankfulness that his life was not in danger. That day, the journal entry of "Worried about Craig's shoulder" moved from *On my heart* to *Peace*—"Craig does not have a tumor."

Of course, the next months were emotionally difficult for Craig and Lara as they adjusted to his baseball career ending before it began. That adjustment became a new topic in my journal where, again, I could see God moving through a difficult situation and answering prayer after prayer. Craig and Lara were married in December of 1993. Both are happily pursuing their careers. Craig's is based on other interests and skills completely unrelated to baseball. Lara is a freelance writer.

I sometimes look back in my journal and more clearly remember the goodness of God in their lives. Those journal entries shine a light on the process from anxiousness to peace. They are a written confirmation of a passage written by the apostle Paul:

> Be anxious for nothing, but in everything
> by prayer and supplication, with thanksgiving,
> let your requests be made known to God; and
> the peace of God, which surpasses all
> understanding, will guard your hearts and
> minds through Christ Jesus.
>
> —Philippians 4:6-7

What we write down doesn't matter as much as the fact that we write. It is a matter of reflection. I often think I have a sense of God speaking to me or prompting me to ponder something. If I don't write it down, I may lose it. Other times, I sense insight to some matter and know that I need to sit and think through what I am sensing. Journaling helps me do that.

Even if we only make journal entries infrequently, they can serve to unravel the tangle of changes pulsing through our lives. Write anything. It is for you and God. He can handle whatever you write. He may even use it as a way to allow you to hear Him more clearly.

Bible Reading and Prayer

As committed Christians, we have all been taught to have devotions. Many of us probably read the Bible daily, and for many people prayer is like breathing. These disciplines feed our spirit. They can also provide a needed anchor in times of chaos and distressing physical symptoms. Even if prayer and devotion don't take away the symptoms, they can provide the stability to know that we are not alone, even in this changing time of life.

It is during this season that many seasoned Christian women feel that their time with the Lord is "flat." The women in my focus groups said that they didn't end their devotion times feeling any better than when they began. They didn't have the enthusiasm for Bible reading and prayer that they used to have.

"My spiritual resources were powerless," Carol said. "I had always been able to draw on the Lord in times of stress; but when the emotional attacks I experienced came, it didn't work."

Other women agreed with Carol that they felt like they were groping in the dark for what was once readily available. These women realized that their spiritual fog was another symptom of learning to cope with both physical and chemical changes.

They also realized that God understood how they felt and was with them. He was not requiring them to pull themselves up by the bootstraps and charge ahead. He gave them the freedom to muddle around a bit and know that He still loved them. Even if they didn't always feel

Date: _____

This is how menopause affected my marriage (or a personal relationship) ...

the emotions that spurred them on in the past, they understood the value of continuing in Bible reading and prayer.

Meditation

While most of us are quite familiar with how to read the Bible and pray, we may be novices at meditation. In fact, the very term may conjure up negative feelings. I am not suggesting meditation in any way like the New Age practice. Richard Foster, in his book *Celebration of Discipline,* explains the difference:

> All Eastern forms of meditation stress the need to become detached from the world. There is an emphasis upon losing personhood and individuality and merging with the Cosmic Mind. ... Personal identity is lost in a pool of cosmic consciousness. ... Detachment is the final goal of Eastern religion.
>
> Christian meditation goes far beyond the notion of detachment ... we must go on to *attachment.* The detachment from the confusion all around us is in order to have a richer attachment to God and to other human beings.[1]

I don't practice meditation regularly or in a very structured way. I do my own thing. And my own thing is very simple. I take the phone off the hook. I sit in our sunroom at the back of the house, surrounded by windows and breathtaking views of the mountains. I read a short passage of Scripture, close my eyes, and wait. I sit there for a few minutes and try to focus on the words I've read.

Sometimes I'm impressed by something very specific. One morning I was sitting with my eyes closed, enjoying the warmth of the sun, and thinking on the words *Christ's love.* For a few days prior to this time, I had been concerned about whether I would ever know anything about my heritage. I had only known about my adoption for about a year, but I had no specific information. While focusing on the words *Christ's love,* I was struck with the thought that I didn't need to worry at all about finding out about my past. The Lord would reveal what He wanted me to know in due time. I could almost hear God say, "I love you and will tell you details about your past. Don't worry."

"I have come that they might have life and have it to the full."
—*John 10:10 (NIV)*

Sometimes I am not impressed with any specific thought. But there is still a sense of connection with God and a peacefulness that I seldom experience elsewhere in the hectic pace of life.

An example of a passage I like to meditate on is this:

> For this reason I bow my knees to the Father of our Lord Jesus Christ, from whom the whole family in heaven and earth is named, that He would grant you, according to the riches of His glory, to be strengthened with might through His Spirit in the inner man, that Christ may dwell in your hearts through faith; that you, being rooted and grounded in love, may be able to comprehend with all the saints what is the width and

> length and depth and height—to know the
> love of Christ which passes knowledge; that
> you may be filled with all the fullness of God.
> —Ephesians 3:14-19

When I sit in my sunroom, with the majesty of the Rocky Mountains before me, and think quietly on this passage, I am overwhelmed. I am struck with how incomprehensible the love of God is. I leave from moments like those with the reassurance that I really am loved far more than I can imagine. It is renewing.

Another Scripture that I can meditate on for many days is:

> Finally, brethren, whatever things are true,
> whatever things are noble, whatever things are
> just, whatever things are pure, whatever things
> are lovely, whatever things are of good report,
> if there is any virtue and if there is anything
> praiseworthy—meditate on these things.
> —Philippians 4:8

Dream Again

"What are your dreams?" I asked one focus group.

"Things don't thrill me like they used to," Nancy replied. She once had dreams that excited her, but she hadn't thought about them for years.

Penny expressed similar feelings, "I don't have a big desire to do too much. I feel kind of lazy."

We talked about how it is so hard to figure out "what I want to be when I grow up." When we were young, we could dream more enthusiastically because we still had lots of time to accomplish them. For some of us, our

131

dreams were focused on raising our children with little attention to what we might dare attempt after they were grown. So by this stage, our empty nests may feel more like holes in our hearts.

I have always loved the verse, "Therefore we also, since we are surrounded by so great a cloud of witnesses, let us lay aside every weight, and the sin which so easily ensnares us, and let us run with endurance the race that is set before us" (Hebrews 12:1).

But when my younger daughter left home, I found I had no finish line in view for the race I was to run. I couldn't decide what God wanted me to do or what I thought I could do. I still have moments when the ribbon across the finish line is blurred. Discouragement comes when I feel too old to pursue dreams.

It's Not Too Late

I remember being in a seminar where Florence Littauer was the keynote speaker. She gave a talk based on her book *Silver Boxes: The Gift of Encouragement*. It is a wonderful story about her father who didn't accomplish some of his dreams because of a lack of encouragement. But he gave the gift of encouragement to Florence. In another one of her books, *Dare to Dream*, she says,

> I try to give each one hope by saying "It's never too late to dare to dream. I didn't write my first book until I was almost fifty. Get moving!" I'm convinced from the overwhelming response I've received from *Silver Boxes* that almost everyone has a latent desire within them that has not been fulfilled.[2]

132

I have always been a big dreamer. But I must agree with some of the women in the focus groups. It is harder to be excited about new endeavors in the midst of mid-life circumstances.

I have spent many hours, usually before drifting off to sleep, thinking about pursuing meaningful dreams. One thought that comes back repeatedly is that when I feel good physically, I feel enthusiastic about running a new race. But when I feel bad physically, I don't feel like doing anything. I am convinced that once the physical symptoms of menopause are over, there will be a renewed vision for life.

For those of us in the middle of the process, we need to hang on during the tough part. This is one reason why I find that taking a few quiet minutes to think about the future is comforting—and even exciting. I allow my mind to wonder:

> *Play is the exultation of the possible.*
> *—Martin Buber*

If I could do anything at all and be sure of success, what would I do?

My most frequent answer is that I would love to write and speak with such power that teeming masses would read or hear my words and their lives would be changed. They would be sincerely encouraged about themselves and their lives, and they would be enticed to long for an intimate relationship with Jesus. In my dreams, my books sell millions and I speak to packed stadiums.

Reality hasn't caught up with my dreams yet, but I am

drawn on by the image of a future in which I continue to run the race set before me.

What is *your* dream?

Something Bubbling

When I found my primary role in life changing from parent to parent-of-adult-children, I suffered a sense of loss and confusion. But I also felt a bubbling excitement pushing its way up into my consciousness. In the middle of all the frustrations and choices of mid-life, there was an exuberant, inner urging to reach back and play with some long-ago forsaken treasures.

For me, this play results in pockets of time where I enjoy life for the sheer joy of it. I sit and play the piano, even though I can't play well. I fiddle with the familiar pieces and don't bother with perfecting them for anyone else to hear. I ride up into the mountains and eat lunch at a quaint Swiss restaurant and remember wonderful trips to other countries. I go to a local coffeehouse, where a lot of college students hang out, and pretend I'm in a Paris café. And I am planning to ice skate again. I loved to skate growing up and dreamed of being an Olympic competitor. I haven't skated in over eight years, and now I want to put on my olds skates just to see how they feel. I feel no pressure to be a champion, only a desire to enjoy the sound of the blade on the ice and remember many happy times.

Julia Cameron, in her book *The Artist's Way,* talks about this revival of our creative energies:

> We begin to excavate our buried dreams.
> This is a tricky process. Some of our dreams
> are very volatile, and the mere act of brushing
> them off sends an enormous surge of energy
> bolting through our denial system. Such grief!
> Such loss! Such pain! ... We mourn the self we
> abandoned.[3]

But what joy to dabble in pursuits that delight our souls. I know several women who have begun to do just that. One has begun to paint again after over twenty years. She paints for her own enjoyment and pleasure. Another has started a class in a foreign language. Others write poetry, pick up a discarded musical instrument and play again, read extensively on a topic of interest just for the fun of it, or embark on a host of other adventures.

The Presence of God

None of these pursuits are antithetical to the pursuit of God. Of course, any of them could be misused and turned into a barrier to seeking God. But I have found that I often see God more clearly when I allow myself this kind of free-spirited play and find my spiritual insight is sharpened.

When I ride up to the mountains, I see God's benediction all around me. Gliding across the floor of an ice rink transports me to a place of physical freedom where the hindrances to movement fall off and I soar. In those moments, my soul soars, too.

So often in seeking God we limit our search to the known and routine.

So often in seeking God we limit our search to the known and routine. We segregate our spiritual lives into the times we are reading the Bible, praying, or attending church. There is a great spiritual reality in enjoying life in ways that express ourselves as God has made us. We don't abandon the known and routine.

> *Our minds need relaxation, and give way / Unless we mix with work a little play.*
> —Moliere

We become more balanced. Most of us are pretty tightly wound and fearful of being too frivolous. The second half of life can become so much more joyful if we launch out a little. And launching out doesn't mean we're moving away from God. He comes with us, and He gives us the incredible riches of His grace to enjoy His world and our existence in it.

A Word of Encouragement

Relaxation may not be a part of your life now. It may seem unlikely that you can squeeze it into your busy schedule. But, try just a few things suggested in this chapter: soak in a hot tub, sit in a sunny room, and daydream for a few minutes.

You may find yourself feeling invigorated after this kind of break. Hopeful thoughts for your future will begin to blossom. The value of nurturing yourself will help move relaxation breaks into your schedule. You'll love this addition to your life. Give it a try.

Hello—

I'm hiding in the kitchen with the ladies.

The idea of facilitating an all-male focus group

has me on edge.

Wishing I weren't here—

Lois

CHAPTER 9

I Don't Want to Talk to Men About Menopause

I didn't want to interview any men for this book.

"Are you kidding?" I responded when my publisher— yes, a man—said he wanted a section on what men think about menopause.

"I already know what men think," I protested.

Men think menopausal women are powder kegs about to explode at the least jostle. Men make jokes about women aging and being hysterical and looking awful and forgetting their own names and sweating buckets and talking in rambling sentences ...

My mind flashed back to an encounter I had with a male friend. I was sitting on the floor of a local Christian bookstore, looking through the women's section to see what was already published on menopause. I heard a familiar voice say, "Lois, is that you?"

I looked up to see Tony, the husband of a woman I know.

"Hi, Tony!"

"What are you up to?" he asked. "You look pretty intent."

"Oh," I said as I got up from my studious position. "I'm doing a book and checking out what's already been written on the subject."

"What's the book about?" he asked.

"Well," I replied, lowering my voice so no one else could hear, "it's about women and mid-life." I couldn't bring myself to utter the word *menopause.*

> *Women wish to be loved without a why or a wherefore; not because they are pretty, or good, or well-bred, or graceful, or intelligent, but because they are themselves.*
> *—Henri Frederic Amiel*

I couldn't believe it. He blushed. He shuffled, he looked down, and finally he said, "Lois, if you write a book on *that,* you'll end up going around the country *talking* about it."

Tony changed the subject. We stayed on safe topics until it seemed natural for him to leave. As soon as he was out of sight, I turned and hurried out of the store.

I felt ashamed. Ashamed! Why did I feel like I had done something shameful? His response seemed to verify what I thought I knew about how men think about menopause—it's too embarrassing to even talk about.

Webster defines *shame* as "a painful feeling of having lost the respect of others because of the improper behavior, incompetence, of oneself or another." I think women feel like their behavior during menopause causes men to lose respect for them. They believe they are seen as frantic females who cannot control themselves.

I argued with my publisher that all women, not just me, knew what men thought. He persisted. Steve agreed with him. They outnumbered me.

Men, I thought sullenly. *What do they know about how women feel about this touchy subject? Why would women want to read about the jokes the men are telling?*

What Husbands Say

I thought about getting together a focus group in the same way I had interviewed women, but I was nervous about calling these men. I didn't want to explain the concept of a group of men getting together to talk about menopause.

So I called one of the more sensitive men that I know. He is a counselor and natural encourager. He and his wife are in their late forties, so I thought he would have contact with men in the right age group. Paul was wonderful. He agreed to get a group of men together at his house for an evening group that I would facilitate. The only requirement for these men was that their wives had started to have some of the symptoms of menopause.

The day of the group meeting arrived, and I almost called it off. I felt really vulnerable at the thought of me and all these men talking about the "M" word. The wives had decided to gather at another house while I interviewed their husbands. When I arrived at Paul's home, I was grateful that his wife and a few of the other wives were still there. But as they left, I felt more strongly than ever that I should be going with them instead of staying with the men.

Despite my apprehension, the evening was great. The men were kind, comfortable, and eager to help. I began by asking them how they felt about what their wives were going through.

Mike

Mike, who was the oldest, began with an admission that he had not been very sensitive when his wife had gone through menopause.

"I was a fifties kind of guy in a nineties setting," he said. "I remember not being very aware of what was going on."

Mike's wife was past menopause, so his presence at the meeting was an encouragement to the other men. The rest of them expressed knowing very little, or thinking very little, about menopause before their wives had started to display early symptoms.

Ted

Ted, whose wife had very few symptoms, said that he was apprehensive about his wife entering menopause because of what he had heard years ago in college. He had a professor who told his classes that his wife went through the change and divorced him. Ted admitted that he had no other information on menopause.

Scott

Scott said that he really had no idea what to expect either as his wife began to have some symptoms. The only thing he had noticed so far was that his wife was nervous about her loss of memory.

"I told her," Scott said, "*I* must have been going through menopause for the last ten years—my memory is gone.

"I want to be supportive, but I really don't know what to say. I want to be an authority, but I am not."

> *Love is that condition in which the happiness of another person is essential to your own.*
> *—Robert A. Heinlein*

Dwayne

Dwayne sat listening to the other men talk with pensive interest. He told the group that he and his wife are on the front part of being there with a capital "T." *There* describes mid-life with all of its changes—retirement, new job, kids leaving, physical changes for him and his wife.

141

"I don't feel very attached to her problem," Dwayne said, referring to his wife's decisions on how to handle menopausal symptoms, "which is strange for me. I am more intrigued and fascinated with what is happening to my eternally youthful wife and the impact that is going to have at a time of transition in my own life."

Dwayne went on to tell how he had learned to recognize when his wife wanted to be left alone. He knew that she meant nothing against him and only wanted to handle her feelings in her own way.

Several men agreed with Dwayne that they felt like spectators. They watched and cared, but didn't know what to do.

Matt

Matt had been divorced before his current marriage and feels he learned a lot the first time around. His first wife, though not at the age of menopause, had emotional mood swings. When she did, Matt would detach because he felt hurt and beat up. Now, in his current marriage, he feels he better understands the role emotions play in menopause. He and his wife have been able to connect emotionally. He attributes that connection to his experience in his first marriage, his increased knowledge as a result of becoming a counselor, and his wife's ability to handle difficulties well.

Paul

"I think there is a correlation between menopause for women and hair loss for men," Paul said as he ran his

142

hand over his smooth, shiny head. A few other comments about waistline bulges confirmed that these men were beginning to experience their own mid-life symptoms.

Paul continued, "I think we don't talk about menopause because it has to do with sex. There is a taboo in talking about it."

Paul is also a counselor and talks to a lot of women who are suffering from menopausal symptoms. He said he tries to be supportive of them and encourages them to speak up. He thinks the public needs to be educated so that women with symptoms will address them.

New Ideas and New Experiences

Surprisingly, the men in this focus group were as comfortable and supportive as the women had been. Their comments reflected how the topic had opened up some new thoughts for them:

Dwayne: "My attitudes are that it is her [my wife] going through this passage, and I view me as stationary. And yet, when I look at it realistically, I realize I am *there*. There is a solemnity in me. Proof to me that we are in another season of life. This is serious stuff."

Matt: "I think it has to do with nurturing. When our wives are ill, we need to be nurturing, and these are not natural things for us. God has really been putting us [husbands] through some maturing and growing so we can be there for them at this stage of life."

Scott: "It is a real learning process for women. Emotions are high, but it is because of going through menopause, retirement, empty nest. There is a lot going on. Women try to compare with other women."

Paul: "The problem is when we make comparisons, it is a criticism. Part of my anger is that when we go through stages, we don't deal very well with losses. When society values youth and values women for beauty and childbearing, I think women need support [as they perceive these losses and grieve them]. I bought a plaque when we moved here, *Come grow old with me, the best is yet to be.* It really should be that way—trying to be sensitive about losses."

Paul's comments about beauty and comparison led to a discussion about the pressure put on women to remain physically attractive. One of the men said that he and his wife enjoy wonderful, intimate times and that she is still very sexually attractive to him. Yet she worries about having put on a few pounds and not looking like a model.

They agreed that the loss of physical beauty is difficult and that they want to be affirming and encouraging to their wives. They admitted that seeing their wives deal with physical changes caused them to think more about their own aging process.

"I can't run as far or as fast as I used to. My hair is thinning. My waist is thicker," Paul said as the others nodded their heads in agreement.

"I can't read a thing without my glasses," someone else said.

"I am winded much quicker than I used to be," Matt added.

Date: _____

RECEIVED

When I experienced menopause, (choose one)

☐ the people living at home were affected in these ways …

☐ I had a freshly emptied nest. This is how I felt about that adjustment …

☐ I had no children in the home. Were that NOT the case, this is how I would want someone to pray for me …

Someone finally ventured a question about sex after menopause. "What will happen down the road sexually to my wife? Will we end up in separate bedrooms? Some of you are *there*. What's it like?"

"If people are loving and communicating," Paul answered, "things are fine."

Someone else chimed in that the couples at mid-life might not continue to have sex as frequently, which caused Mike (the menopause veteran in the group) to grin broadly. Then the rest of the group started to smile, as if to say it had been some years since most of them had been as sexually active as in their youth. No one else said anything more, but they seemed content to trust that their wives would not be moving out of their bedrooms.

I wish we had had this conversation five years ago. I have learned more from my peers than I could have imagined. — Dwayne, husband of menopausal wife

By the end of the evening, Dwayne summarized the sentiment in the room. "I wish we had had this conversation five years ago. I have learned more from my peers than I could have imagined. I would not talk like this on the golf course or anywhere. Has anyone ever heard a man mention that his wife is going through menopause? Never. Men don't talk about it and [yet talking about] it is so helpful. What I have concluded is that I shouldn't be so passive as I am now and pay more attention to what my wife is going through. I'm going to encourage discussion and share myself more."

As I folded up my laptop to head for home, someone asked eagerly, "What do they say about us? What do they want us to do?"

And that is the subject of the next chapter.

A Word of Encouragement

Most husbands want to be helpful and supportive. Sometimes they don't know how. As you go through this life passage and talk with your spouse, be encouraged by the responses of the men in this chapter. If he seems shaken at first, keep in mind that these changes unsettle him—just as they unsettle you. Both of you need time to think and adjust. And you need time to talk.

As a couple, you can love each other more deeply and grow closer if you approach the issues of menopause together. Sharing brings understanding or, at least, common bewilderment at this perplexing time of life.

The focus group went well, yet my heart is saddened a bit for Rhonda. She told her story about dating in mid-life, and though she had us in stitches, I still grieve for her. I know many women in her shoes wish they weren't here—

Lois

CHAPTER 10

What Wives Wish Their Husbands Knew and a Mindset Metamorphosis for Every Grown-Up

"Men want to fix everything," one woman told her group. "I just want him to hold me and tell me he still loves me."

Her sentiments ring true for many women.

There is no easy fix for every problem that vexes the menopausal woman.

While *some* things can be done to alleviate *some* physical symptoms, it's the emotional effects that have women—and men—so bewildered. Combine these two—the physical changes and the emotional ups and downs—and you have a situation that can frustrate a marriage and challenge a woman's identity as a sexual being.

He who loveliness within Hath found, all outward loathes, For he who color loves, and skin, Loves but their oldest clothes.
—John Donne

For married women, the comments below will resonate. Further on, we'll see how the mental transition from the childbearing age to the grandchildren-rearing stage does not change—but rather enhances—femininity.

What Wives Wish Their Husbands Knew

More than having their menopause problems "fixed," women want to know that their husbands will stay connected to them, or begin connecting with them, and walk through this stage of life together.

"Don't give a lot of advice," another woman responded when asked about what she tells her husband she needs. "I want to be able to say how I feel—without feeling like I have to take his advice."

This woman may sound ungrateful, but she is only frustrated. Like so many husbands, her man wants to help. Yet his attempts to fix her only frustrate her.

It is difficult for men to accept that they can do nothing to make menopausal symptoms go away. There are, however, many ways husbands can provide the one

thing these women truly need: support. And that support
will be awfully hard to offer if they don't accept certain
rules of encountering menopause moments.

Be Assured that Emotional Symptoms Are (Usually) Caused by Physiological Changes, Not by Husbands

One woman said, "My husband never knows exactly
what he'll find when he gets home from work. Some days
I'm my normal self, which is pretty calm. Other days, I
am off the wall. I am agitated and tearful. He comes in,
and I just light right into him. I don't mean to take my
frustration out on him, but I do."

The women I interviewed agreed that husbands should
be assured that they are rarely the true cause of emotional
outbursts, but they may often be the recipients. Now
that's a tall order: asking men to bear the brunt of
fluctuating emotions—without taking it personally.
But if they don't, they may be hurt in ways their wives
never intended.

Steve and I talked about how to get through the times I
felt like an emotional basket case. He tried not to be
detached, but rather to verbalize that he was sorry I felt
bad and that he was there for me. I would do my best to
remember that he didn't cause my feelings and that this
trying time would pass. He didn't pressure me to change;
and most importantly, I allowed myself some time alone
to regain my composure.

Of course, couples can have interpersonal problems that
cause emotional distress completely unrelated to
menopause. There may be stress over adjusting to issues

such as children leaving home, caring for elderly parents, finances, and retirement. These issues need to be addressed with reference to whatever is the root cause of the problem—communication, self-worth, and more.

Don't Make Fun of Menopausal Women

Women don't want to be the object of jokes. A sense of humor is fine, but jokes or remarks about being old or menopausal won't build relationships—especially when these comments are made in front of other people. Most couples are able to laugh together privately about some of the strange behaviors women demonstrate, but only after the symptoms causing the behavior have passed. Steve and I would often joke about my forgetfulness (you'll hear about it from him in the next chapter), but this occurred privately, not while I was frantically looking for a vanished item.

Validate That Symptoms Are Real

In the same way that women don't want their suffering to be mocked or minimized through jokes, they do want their feelings validated. They don't want to be dismissed as hysterical or suffering from some imaginary dysfunction. They don't want to be told that their symptoms are cases of mind over matter—change your mind and the matter will change.

Husbands can communicate their support by being willing to read a book or an article that explains menopause. They don't need to be experts, but their interest is very encouraging.

Support New Interests

Many women are venturing out into new territory
during the mid-life years. A woman may go back to work
for the first time in years. She may go back to school or
pick up an old interest with new enthusiasm. It is
wonderful to be asked about any new area with sincere
interest. These conversations are not unlike dinner
conversations where men talk about their time at work.
A woman is deeply encouraged when her husband
remembers and is willing to spend time talking about
her interests.

These newfound interests may also require that her
husband make some accommodations. If she's the family
chef, he may forego a home-cooked meal for take-out if
she has a class. He may delay purchasing a new power
tool to buy her a sewing machine or other hobby tools.
Whatever the sacrifice, she'll appreciate his endorsement
as she transitions to this new season.

Remain Faithful

There are too many stories of men who have mid-life
crises and decide to leave their wives. This term is often
used to explain why men become involved with younger
women. Unfortunately a man's mid-life crisis often
coincides with a woman's menopause.

An article in *Woman's Day* quoted a rise in the
percentage of divorces after the age of fifty-five due, in
part, to this very reason:

> They enter their golden years and their
> husband walks out the door, often for a

younger woman. That's what's happening to an increasing number of women in their fifties and sixties these days. While divorce among younger people seems to be leveling off, there's a worrisome rise in marriage breakups among the over-fifty-five crowd—up 22 percent in the last decade and expected to climb.[1]

As these women grapple with feelings of low self-esteem and inadequacy, their husbands wrestle with their own feelings of inadequacy. Most women I interviewed whose husbands had extra-marital affairs said privately that they were unaware of how their husbands felt until it was too late. The affairs had already occurred as their husbands sought to have their needs met superficially in relationships with other women.

> *Mid-life can be a rough time for both men and women, but a solid commitment to weather the storms together will help solve problems.*

Mid-life can be a rough time for both men and women, but a solid commitment to weather the storms together will help solve problems. Unfaithfulness by either men or women will only create many more painful problems.

Ask Questions, Really Listen, and Respond

Women want their husbands to talk to them. They want their husbands to risk asking them how they feel. Husbands might encounter differing responses to that question—emotional reactions, withdrawal, confusion, appreciative answers—but, whatever the response, most women appreciate interest in how they feel.

"My problem," Marie said, "is that my husband will ask me how I feel, then he won't really listen to what I say. He asks me as he is walking into the other room, or glancing at the paper, or shuffling through the mail. So I answer and that is the end of the conversation. His question was not sincere."

A helpful sequence goes like this: Ask, listen, respond. Husbands who say they don't know how to respond, should simply confess, "I don't know what to say, but I want to try to understand."

Women want to know they are cared for and cared about. They want to know that their husbands think about them. For women, that means discussing the aging processes relevant to themselves and their husbands.

Reframing Sexuality: Mindset Metamorphosis for Every Grown-Up

Thus far, the focus of this discussion has been on what wives wish their husbands knew. But menopause is no respecter of females. Women, married or not, have to face relationship and self-image challenges that are not exclusive to marriage. The simple fact that we are sexual creatures—created male and female by God's choosing—brings in a whole other batch of complications that seem magnified (at least to us) as we fear we're losing our essence of femininity.

Fortunately, that is not the case. We'll see shortly that our sexuality does not wane with our estrogen.

The Challenging Mix of Dating and Menopause

I know from personal experience that dating as an adult can be difficult. Add the onset of menopause and it can be a calamity. Imagine being with a man you find attractive and suddenly you're sweating into your shrimp cocktail. Or he asks you what happened at work that day, and you can't remember. To makes things worse, there's always the chance that a younger bombshell will come on the scene, and in a moment of self-comparison and internalized competition, you push yourself over the edge and into an anxiety attack.

And heaven forbid if you have an unexplained mood swing in the middle of a first date. Unless he grew up in a house full of hormonal sisters, you may have sealed your fate with that man forever. I mean, if husbands have tough times understanding wives that they've lived with for decades, I can sympathize with dating males who strive to be charming in the face of menopause.

Then, of course, I can also sympathize with the menopausal woman who has to deal with a less-than-charming date, whose innocent comments can bring painful mid-life issues to the fore.

Rhonda had one such experience:

"My last date was a real nightmare. There was no seat on the passenger side of his car, and I had to move fishing poles to get in the back seat."

Rhonda, full of humor and drama, told how she spent the evening listening to her date complain about the cost of every item on the menu—of the restaurant *he* had selected. In between complaints, he spoke about himself. Then when he dropped her off at her house, he began to talk about wanting to get married and have children.

Rhonda is in her late forties and has had a hysterectomy.

"It was the first time I mourned the loss of my parts," she said to an already smiling group of women. With her reference to "parts," we all broke into roars of laughter, including Rhonda.

Her date worsened with the poignant reminder that she wasn't young enough to provide what many men want. This particular man would, undoubtedly, not have been a marriage candidate for Rhonda even if she had been much younger. But his desire for children isn't all that uncommon.

> *"The LORD does not look at the things man looks at. Man looks at the outward appearance, but the LORD looks at the heart."*
> *—1 Samuel 16:7b (NIV)*

Many single women are able to listen to dating stories like Rhonda's and laugh because they are past the game-playing stage. Most accept themselves and are not interested in trying to become what men want. They are themselves. If they meet men who appreciate them for who they are, great. If not, they are not willing to try to be someone else's fantasy.

On the other hand, single, middle-aged men are in a tough spot, too. They have their own pains and issues of mid-life to handle in addition to deciding how to relate to women. Successful dating relationships in the mid-life years depend on the maturity of the people involved. Mature men and women can enjoy meaningful relationships if they are able to be themselves and accept others as they are also.

Feelings of Threatened Sexuality

Women who are grappling with signs of physical aging often feel like their very sexuality is threatened. They think they are regarded by others as unsexy, and while they may not subscribe to this perception *personally*, they may regard themselves as un-sexual, meaning they feel less feminine than before. Our culture tangles sexuality (the comprehensive quality of femininity or masculinity) with sexiness (the erotic quality of arousing sexual desire). It is important to see the distinction.

God created Eve female; she remained female all her life. She didn't reach mid-life and suddenly turn into an asexual being. Likewise, we who are born female remain female until we die. Our sexuality continues to be expressed throughout our lives. Certainly the end of childbearing years marks a change in one expression of our sexuality. But this change does not void our driver's license—the description *female* still applies.

The characteristics of mid-life sexuality expressed by the Christian women in the focus groups included contentment, acceptance, graciousness, kindness. These qualities reflect a woman who understands, in some small way, what it means to be in the presence of her Creator who sees her as completely feminine, no matter what her vintage.

What we lose as we age is not our sexuality; it is only the physical body of youth. What the world calls *sexy* does fade away. Who we are as sexual beings remains with us all the days of our lives.

"My, I'm Thinking Differently Now!"

One woman in the focus groups said, "I've heard that there are three stages of life: youth, mid-life, and 'My you're looking well.'"

We all laughed at her sarcastic reference to "looking well," and then we remembered the days when the word *well* meant "pretty," "beautiful," or even "fantastic." Most of us felt the sting of fading from the ranks of the physically-praised and moving to the sidelines of the cosmetically-concealed. We knew that the telltale compliment that marks this move is, *You are looking great, for a woman your age.*

Living in a society that so worships physical, sexual perfection, it is difficult to change from valuing our physical appeal to valuing our inner beauty. However, things are a little better than they were a decade ago: Women are valued for more than winning beauty pageants. Some are moving into high-ranking professional positions as a result of their qualifications, not their looks. They are more frequently written about in magazines and newspapers for their accomplishments.

In spite of these changes for the better, the media still touts the youthful and well-built female, one with big breasts, a small waist, shapely hips, long legs, wrinkle-free skin, silky hair, and a fat-free body. That ideal places incredible pressure on girls and young women, but for women in their forties or fifties, it completely slips from the realm of possibility.

> *Gray hair is a crown of splendor; it is attained by a righteous life.*
> *—Proverbs 16:31 (NIV)*

The women I interviewed were at different stages of acceptance regarding physical aging and their self-concepts of sexuality. The very first group I talked with surprised me with their responses. I asked a question about the cosmetic industry targeting mid-life women with anti-aging products.

"We're too smart to fall for that kind of advertising," one woman replied.

The others agreed that they had long ago given up running after the elusive goal of the physically perfect woman. These women were enjoying a self-acceptance that was not shared by the groups I interviewed later on.

"It is just so hard to catch my reflection in a mirror and see that I am not as young as I feel I am," said Terry, an attractive woman in her late forties. "I used to get a lot of compliments on how good I looked. That doesn't happen so often anymore."

The realities of mid-life and aging—weight gain, wrinkles, sagging bodies, gray hair—may cause us to feel badly about ourselves. So how can we change our thinking about our sexuality?

We accept that we are not sexy young things. And we remind ourselves that our sexuality—our Creator's choice to make us female—is not about attracting men with physical beauty. It is about accepting who we are and how we look, and pursuing the purposes to which God has called us as women. As we discover and consider the differences between *sexy* and *sexuality*, we will grow to be more comfortable with ourselves in light of the physical changes in our bodies.

For me, the changes in menopause have made me a softer, more feminine person than I was a few years ago. I don't react to situations with sarcasm. I accept differing opinions more graciously. I also know that I look older, my face has more wrinkles, and my waist is a little thicker. But I believe that my sexuality is more readily perceived in my softer personality than it used to be with my younger look.

Thinking about our sexuality means letting go of old images of the sexy female. It means appreciating the qualities of mature beauty, where a few wrinkles surround a smile or gray hair highlights a kind face. It also means giving men more credit than we sometimes do. Many godly men appreciate women as they get older, and they respect women's sexuality in godly ways. That contributes to a woman feeling cherished, appreciated, and worthwhile long after she has lost the world's outer trappings of beauty.

A Word of Encouragement

God sees each of us with loving, fatherly eyes. He looks beneath the surface and into our hearts. He lives in us through His Son and the Holy Spirit. When we think of ourselves in that context, the world's ideas regarding sexuality dim in comparison.

This is what I did to help my husband (or a close friend or relative) understand

my menopause …

Date: _____

RECEIVE

Steve—

Menopause hasn't been easy, but your loving support has been a tremendous help. Thank you so much. Wishing I weren't here (but since I am, I'm so glad it's with you!)—

Lois

CHAPTER 11

Some Things Husbands Wish They Knew
by Steve Rabey

From the very first moment little boys realize there are such things as little girls, males are engaged in a lifelong process of trying to understand and navigate the many mysteries of females.

Some of these mysteries revolve around the many ways females are different from males. Boys realize pretty quickly that girls look different, act different, and smell different. Later on, boys begin to realize that girls think different, too.

These intellectual differences can be so significant some boys conclude that whatever it is girls do "up there," thinking isn't the right name for it. Sadly, some men persist in this belief until their dying day, though that's getting tougher in an age when female students consistently outnumber and outperform male students in colleges and graduate schools.

The realization that males and females love differently typically dawns during the teen years when childhood crushes give way to something more mature. Teen boys may think their own experiences of romance are strange and overpowering, but most teen girls seem to love more deeply, give themselves more completely, and become swept away more fully in their meaningful relationships with boys.

Throughout these many twists and turns in males' accidental education about the sexes, there's one lesson that they find most striking. That lesson is this: Females seem to relate to their own bodies in ways that are completely different from the ways males relate to their bodies.

You can see this difference most clearly in the ways boys and girls play. From the time they realize their own powers of mobility, boys throw themselves into their play with a carefree abandon that females can find shocking. The painful pranks and pratfalls displayed on the *Jackass* TV show and in the movie of the same name demonstrate that this childish abandon can survive well into the so-called adult years. Girls are typically more composed and self-controlled, and as far as I know, there's no regularly broadcast TV show featuring women performing stunts that result in broken bones or other injuries.

But for most of the men I know, menstruation is the mother of all female mysteries and the ultimate symbol of the many differences that separate the boys from the girls. From the first moment they realize that girls have monthly periods until the day they realize that the women in their lives go through menopause, men remain both amazed and confused by the mysteries of the female reproductive system.

When I was 30, I probably would have flunked an easy multiple-choice quiz on the causes and consequences of menopause. Today, having been through what I've been through, I'm supremely confident that I would get at least a C-minus. Along the way there's much I've learned, and in this chapter I hope to share something of a male perspective and some of the more important lessons with women who face menopause and the men who want to love and help them through it.

From the Monastery to the Dorm

I was living a mostly solitary and somewhat Spartan life when I started dating Lois. But that changed rapidly during the first six months of our relationship.

Lara, the younger of Lois's two daughters, was a high school junior when I made my first visit to Lois at her home. It was a Monday evening, and I remember looking forward to seeing Lois, watching a football game on a decent-sized color TV, and eating a home-cooked meal. I was less certain what else might be in store for me during my first foray into Lois's larger familial and social network.

On that evening and on succeeding visits, I remember the feeling of being surrounded by so many women that I occasionally called her house "the dorm." There was Lara and her girlfriends. There was Lois and her girlfriends. And there seemed to be a large and ever-changing parade of people who were mostly girlfriends and boyfriends of the various girlfriends.

Lois always seemed like she knew what was going on in her household, and most of the time it appeared that she was in charge of the proceedings, though her control wasn't always evident to the household's full-time residents and temporary guests.

Still, one of the early images I had of Lois was that she was strong, and maybe even a bit tough. First, she was a firm and loving mother. People often combine the words *firm* and *loving,* but Lois brought these together in a way that was wonderful to behold. She was also a take-charge person who would rather guide things than stand by and passively watch them unfold. Some people might have even thought of Lois as invulnerable.

But the image of a strong and tough Lois began to unravel somewhat as she began to enter menopause. As Lois changed, I changed, too. And as we changed, so did the ways we related to each other.

Forces Beyond Her Control

In the opening chapter of this book Lois described a trip we took to my hometown of Springfield, Ohio. It was the first time I had visited Springfield in a number of years, and my first-ever tour of my old stomping grounds with my new bride in tow. Consequently, I had a long list of people I wanted to see. There was much catching up to do, and many people who wanted to meet Lois.

Lois was more than ready to meet my "homies" and learn a bit more about my old friends and early influences. We wanted to spend some time with my mom and dad. I wanted to visit some of the spiritual mentors who had played a powerful role in shaping my faith. I hoped to touch base with some of my old high school and college friends who still lived in the area. And I also wanted to pop in on some of the people I used to work for.

As soon as we landed at the airport I began putting Lois through the paces. She hung with me as well as she could, but before long I noticed a surprising lack of energy and enthusiasm. Initially I attributed it to a bout of tiredness or shyness. Then before we were more than a day into our visit, she experienced the bloating and bleeding that, unknown to both of us, were the signs of the onset of menopause.

I had been cruising at a rapid speed, blazing a trail through both the Miami Valley and my social calendar. Lois's sudden and mysterious setback was like a flat tire. As our whirlwind ground to a halt and we retreated to our hotel room, I wasn't sure what worried me more: Lois's physical discomfort or her uncertainty about what it was that had brought her low.

The next 24 hours would be a time of shocking discoveries for Lois and growing confusion for me. Once Lois heard the emergency clinic doctor describe her bleeding as the first chapter in her "change of life," she was surprised and not terribly relieved. I didn't really have a clue about what was going on. I didn't know why she wasn't relieved, and she seemed emotionally unready to talk much about it. Unfortunately, I would remain largely clueless until I realized Lois needed me in ways she had never needed me before.

Hide and Seek

The sunroom on the back side of our home in Colorado offers great views of the Rocky Mountains and a wonderful spot for watching the finches and bluebirds that gather around the birdfeeder.

It's a great place for sitting, or thinking, or having a cup of coffee, or reading the newspaper. I was doing all four when Lois approached me one morning a few months after our return from Ohio. Her voice had a slightly menacing tone that made me wish I could wrap the newspaper around me like a protective shield.

"Steve!" she said, enunciating my name with a shrill, high-pitched sound. It sounded like a challenge.

"Howzitgoin' dear?" I mumbled, forcing my vocal cords into their first appearance of the day.

"Do you know what this is?"

The question caused me to lower my newspaper and look at her. She was holding a dish. Or at least it looked like a dish to me.

"Uhhh," I began, using my lips to help me form my thoughts. But Lois wasn't in any mood for waiting.

"This is a crystal flower dish that was given to me by my mother."

"OK," I said, momentarily relieved that it did not appear I was being formally charged with breaking it or abusing it in any other way. But my relief had been premature.

"You put it in the dishwasher."

"Yes," I said, confident that putting dirty dishes in the dishwasher was an excellent and even commendable thing for husbands to do.

"You NEVER put crystal in the dishwasher," she said in a huff as if she was reminding a moron for the twentieth time that the sun rises every day.

"Why not?" I asked, expecting a simple explanation. Instead I saw Lois's eyes grow as big as saucers and fill with tears. She left the sunroom and stormed off.

At that point, I did what many men—at least men like me—would do in a similar situation. I returned to reading my newspaper. I didn't want to tangle with Lois while she seemed so upset. A few moments of cooling off would do us both good.

When she came back a few moments later, Lois's temperature had risen a few degrees,

"Well, what do you have to say?"

I wasn't sure how to answer. Part of me wanted to rattle off a list of arguments and excuses: Are you sure you can't clean crystal in a dishwasher? Is that what the directions say? Did the dishwasher actually hurt your flower dish? Is this dish really such a big deal?

But if I had been as wise then as I am now, I would have understood that there was more going on here than I realized, and that Lois's thought process had gone something like this:

- Steve put the flower dish in the dishwasher.
- He always thinks he's right, whether it's loading the dishwasher or loading the trunk of the car for a trip.
- He doesn't care about my things.
- He doesn't care about me.
- He doesn't really love me.
- Part of why he doesn't care about me or love me is because I am getting older.

It's possible that the flower dish episode may have also led Lois directly to contemplating the decline of Western civilization or the looming crisis in the heavens caused by our expanding universe. I'm not sure. But as I would gradually learn, discussions about one thing were hardly ever really discussions about *one* thing. Arguments about small things were typically signals of frustration or sadness concerning big things.

Every relationship—whether it's a marriage or a friendship—involves a process of learning to understand the other person and negotiate the differences that stand in the way. In our case, this process was complicated by the reality of menopause, which seemed to be constantly lurking in the shadows, throwing our lives and conversations into often-heated disarray.

One thing I am still learning is to move toward my wife, especially when there's a tension between us. Instead of wrapping myself in a newspaper or whatever else I can find, I'm trying to be more available. That attitude was particularly important during the times when Lois's change of life put a few wobbles in her otherwise steady internal gyroscope.

Every relationship —whether it's a marriage or a friendship— involves a process of learning to understand the other person and negotiate the differences that stand in the way.

Behind the Silence

Thinking back, I can remember how some of the girls I had known as friends while I was growing up had such wildly varying responses to their monthly periods. For Cheryl, her periods seemed to bother her about as much as a hangnail might, and she brushed them off with a simple shrug. For Brandi, her high school years seemed to be punctuated by feelings of anxiety that would peak about a week before her period and would usually be followed by days of horrible cramps that required bed rest and isolation.

I don't recall ever having a conversation with another male about women's periods. And guys don't typically talk about the varied ways menopause affects the women in their lives. I'm not sure why that's the case. Perhaps it's a feeling of uncertainty about what to say. Perhaps it's a sense that a woman's struggles are a private thing and should remain that way. Perhaps it's that nagging suspicion men sometimes have that even after many years and multiple marriage books or Promise Keepers seminars that we just don't understand women very well.

But things are different with Lois and me. The fact that she has written and spoken about the subject and conducted focus-group interviews with men and their wives makes people feel comfortable about bringing up the subject with us. That doesn't mean it's easy for men to talk to me about menopause, but when I ask them they'll talk about it, and their experiences are as varied as can be.

One man said menopause had made his wife feel a sense of sadness and at times even despair. In this case, the onset of menopause began shortly after the last of the couple's three children had gone away to college.

"It was like a double whammy that was emotional and physical," he said. "It was real confusing to me where the emotional side of things—the missing our children—left off and where the menopause began."

This man loved his wife but said there were times when he felt as if he was losing touch with her. "It's like in the movie *The Perfect Storm*," he said. "The waves are coming in and the ship is going down and people are drowning, but you can't save them."

Another man struggled to cope with changing family dynamics as a teenage son and daughter asked what's wrong with mom.

"Doris had always been so strong and steadfast, but in the last year that's started to crumble," he said. "She snaps at the kids over simple things. Or she withdraws into her shell and says she doesn't care about things that I know she cares about. Doris used to be the pillar of our family, but not anymore. I think it's all too much for her some times."

Men said sex had become complicated. Simple discussions could easily derail and turn into arguments. And don't even ask them about fluctuations in their household temperatures and the battles over the thermostat!

"I keep an extra shirt handy in case the house goes cold," said one man. "It's like driving up the Pikes Peak Highway. It can be warm and sunny at the bottom, but at the top it's cold and snowy."

For me, one of the most surprising things was the fluctuation in Lois's emotional state. Lois is one of the most stable and balanced people I know, but during the toughest months she was all over the map. The unpredictability was frustrating, for even the tiniest of things could send her into a rage.

At times she reminded me of an old college friend who had a weakness for gin and tonics. On occasion he would drink himself into a tizzy and begin punching and lunging at his friends. Lois hadn't developed a sudden

171

drinking problem, but there were days when I thought that might have been easier to handle. At least then I would have known what was going on.

"In Sickness and Health"

I can still remember the day Lois and I married. We used traditional wedding vows that included the phrase "in sickness and health." During the wedding rehearsal those words jumped out at me, and I tried to imagine what they might mean as Lois and I entered into this new life together.

I imagined Lois having a bad cold and bringing her blankets and chicken noodle soup. That was easy. I didn't want to think of an older couple I had known. Elsa had developed Alzheimer's disease, and Carl watched in sorrow and fear as one after another aspects of his beloved wife became enveloped in fog and then disappeared.

Nobody ever told me that menopause might be part of the deal, but it's the one "sickness" that nearly every couple is guaranteed to confront in one way or another. Having been through this process with Lois and having talked to other men about their experiences, there are three important lessons I have learned about the ways husbands can love and care for their wives.

In the interests of fairness and honesty, perhaps it would be best not to claim that I have always mastered all of these lessons, particularly in a book where my wife has the last word. But regardless of my own performance, I believe these to be helpful suggestions for men trying to care for the women they love.

Lesson One: Strength in the Midst of Weakness

For some women, menopause brings more than temporary feelings of discomfort. It's a powerful symbol—perhaps the first they've ever experienced—of their own weakness, finitude, and mortality.

Many people say, "You're as young as you feel." But no matter how young you feel, menopause makes many women suddenly feel older and life seem more fragile.

Beginning with our trip to Ohio, Lois's change of life presented me with new opportunities to "be there" for Lois in ways I hadn't been before. That's because she needed me in ways she hadn't before.

Some men feel a temptation to look at menopause as a woman's problem and excuse themselves from playing any role in the changes it brings in its wake. But for us, one of the changes that came along was a slight recalibration of our relationship, particularly in the way we express needs and respond to such requests. These changes have made our relationship richer and stronger.

Lesson Two: Constancy in the Midst of Confusion

If it weren't for the fact that many things remain constant, life would be a supreme hassle. If you travel long distances by plane, your mind and body are thrown out of kilter perhaps for days until your internal clock readjusts to your new locale. And part of the reason events like the 9/11 terrorist attacks are so upsetting is because they destroy things we have come to perceive as normal, and they leave us feeling uncertain about what could happen next.

For many women, menopause is a source of confusion and uncertainty. On the physical level, the reproductive system is changing gears. On the emotional level, moods and feelings can swing up and down with little regard for the realities of the external world. And on the spiritual level, the changes brought about by menopause led many women to reevaluate some of their core beliefs, values, and personal priorities.

> *On the spiritual level, the changes brought about by menopause led many women to reevaluate some of their core beliefs, values, and personal priorities.*

At a time when so many aspects of life seem to be swirling out of control, the last thing women want is for the men in their lives to go all squishy or begin some quixotic quest to find themselves. My advice to men is that if you're planning a mid-life crisis when your wife begins experiencing symptoms of menopause, put off buying the red sports car for a while and concentrate on being there for her.

Lesson Three: Assurance in the Midst of Uncertainty

The end of a woman's reproductive years signals the end to some of the life-giving and nurturing powers that bring many women so much joy and satisfaction. In addition, some women feel that menopause signifies a transition into the final seasons of life. If menopause is not proof that winter has settled in, many feel it's at least a sign that fall is here.

174

For many women, menopause places a new stress on issues like aging and attractiveness. In a culture where TV shows, movies, and popular music are dominated by teenage celebrities with perfectly proportioned "bods," some women feel that they don't measure up, and some worry that their husbands don't love them as much now that they are older.

Men may not be aware that such currents are shifting under the surface, but that doesn't mean they aren't. Perhaps it's best for men to assume that menopause forces women to struggle with these issues in new and powerful ways, and to spend a little extra time and attention on giving them the assurances they need to carry on.

Senior Moments

Long before she starred in the popular TV series *Murder She Wrote,* Angela Lansbury made her movie debut in a 1944 classic called *Gaslight.* It's one of our favorite old-timey movies and one that has provided both of us with some memorable scenes.

Ingrid Bergman won her first Oscar for playing Paula, a weak and vulnerable woman who marries a dashing, romantic man named Gregory Anton (played by Charles Boyer). Without giving away too much of the plot, let me say that Gregory isn't the perfect picture of a loving husband. And during the course of the film, he nearly succeeds in driving Paula completely nutty.

Our version of *Gaslight* plays out like this. Lois prepares a nice snack for herself, and while she isn't looking I hide her treat in the microwave, or in a cupboard. There's a moment when she wonders where she put her snack, but then she looks at me and I give it back to her, or at least most of it.

Some day, hopefully many years from now, Lois may be doing well enough to lose her snacks without my help. And since I'm younger than her by a decade, chances are she'll begin having such senior moments before I do.

We can laugh about this now, but for many people memory loss and other telltale signs of aging are no laughing matter. That's because our culture is hooked on youth.

When we travel together it's interesting for us to look at the varied ways different cultures treat their elderly members. It's safe to say that in many other cultures the elderly get more respect than they do in North America. In many countries around the world, older adults are respected, honored, looked up to, listened to, and considered an important part of family and society. But in North America many older people spend their final years isolated and forgotten in sterile facilities that are many miles from their nearest family members.

Most of us have a generalized fascination with anything new and a mild disregard for anything that's "so five minutes ago." We act as if our favorite two words were "new" and "improved." This attitude stands in opposition to the word of the Lord given to Jeremiah: "Stand at the crossroads and look; ask for the ancient paths, ask where the good way is, and walk in it, and you will find rest for your souls" (Jeremiah 6:16 NIV).

RECEIVE

personal, practical wisdom for your journey

This my worst story from menopause ...

It's true that recent years have brought us a wave of scientific research and technological developments. Things work faster, computers store more data, and DVDs look better than videos.

But the laws of science and technology don't apply to the things of God or the values of human virtues like wisdom and experience that ripen only with age.

Lois and I aren't sure what's going to happen to us as we grow older, but some of the things we've learned and experienced together during the worst moments of her menopause struggles have reminded us of the importance of our commitment to each other, in sickness and in health.

Neither one of us is necessarily looking forward to aging, but at least we know that we will be here for each other no matter what comes our way. And knowing that makes even the scariest future scenarios look more livable.

A Word of Encouragement to Men

We are now long past this phase of life and peace is, once again, restored. Maintaining a long view is essential while in the middle of menopausal years. Even though the whole process can span a number of years, it does come to an end.

And, many moments of calm punctuate the moments of chaos. We have grown ever closer as we've patiently walked with each other and with the Lord through the good and bad times. You, too, will survive.

Greetings from the west side of my Colorado home.
I've spent a lot of time here—in the sunroom—
talking with God throughout this life change. He's
definitely used "the change" to change me!
Wishing the process could be easier!

Lois

CHAPTER 12

Looking for Relief and Power

Before I talk about the spiritual aspects of mid-life, let me share my own spiritual foundation.

I was first introduced to Jesus at a Bible camp when I was thirteen. Sitting around the campfire on a chilly Tuesday night in August somewhere in eastern Pennsylvania, I heard that it was possible to have a relationship with God by inviting His Son into my life as my own personal Savior. The minister leading the evening service talked about forgiveness and reconciliation with God. I understood that Jesus loved me so much that He had taken the payment for my transgressions against God onto himself. I was forgiven and completely accepted by

*Even pain
Pricks to
livelier living.
—Amy Lowell*

God because of Jesus. It was the most touching message I had ever heard, and I prayed to invite this beautiful Jesus into my heart.

He came. I felt His presence that night and I have ever since. I spent many years hearing little more than the salvation invitation I had heard that night at camp. My parents were not Christians then, and the church I attended didn't preach the gospel. But I never felt alone again. I felt that Jesus was with me and understood my every longing.

By my mid-twenties, I had married and become actively involved in a spiritually vibrant church. Our family grew in the knowledge of what it meant to have an authentic relationship with Christ. That faith was dramatically tested in December 1979 when my first husband, Jack, and three other people were killed in a hot-air balloon accident. I witnessed the accident along with my daughters, Lisa and Lara, and with loved ones of the other victims.

The shock of seeing these men die was tempered by the overwhelming reality of eternal life. God's grace that day, and in all the years since, was poured out on us and saturated us with the sweet assurance of our loved ones being in heaven. All three men had accepted Christ as Savior. Eternal life in heaven is their inheritance.

Mid-life: A Time of Spiritual Reflection

In the years since that fateful day, I have continued to experience life lived in relationship with God through faith in His Son and trust in His Holy Spirit.

But when those first early symptoms of menopause hit, something new happened. The emotional ups and downs were different from the emotional responses I had experienced in the past. I began to feel disconnected from everything that had once been familiar. My children were grown and gone. I had remarried, and my marriage was new and unfamiliar. My body was not responding as it always had. I was overwhelmed with a sense of fragmentation.

In all of this, I never stopped praying or relating to God. I knew He was still active in my life. I just *felt* so strange—so distant from everyone. During that time I allowed myself to become much more open with the Lord than I ever had in the past. I expressed my frustration to Him about how I felt and asked Him questions about things I had taken for granted. I wondered about the church and its role in society. I questioned if my own heart was right toward all of God's people, including the poor and disenfranchised. Was I too comfortable in my neat little Christian circle of friends? How should I spend my time, now that my priorities had shifted from being a full-time parent?

These may seem like the aimless ramblings of one hysterical woman, but many of the women I interviewed expressed similar feelings. They were relieved to hear that other Christian women were thinking the same thoughts.

Menopause rocks the boat. It stirs up the emotions and results in much soul-searching. The result for me—and

> *Menopause rocks the boat. It stirs up the emotions and results in much soul-searching.*

for many other women—has been a deeper, much more personal faith. God seems bigger. He is not only defined by doctrine and theology; He is defined by person-to-person encounters in the quiet of questioning hearts. The questions are about living lives of significance. What is truly important? What does God want us to do differently? How can we better love Him? It is a freeing time to look again at what we believe and reevaluate how to reflect the reality of Christ in our lives in unique and personal ways.

Women Seeking Spiritual Answers

Christian women are not unique in their mid-life spiritual thoughts. Many secular books and articles attest to the fact that menopause involves a spiritual dimension. These writings seek to apply spiritual remedies to relieve symptoms, inspire meaning in life, and accept death.

Over twenty million women in the U.S. alone will enter menopause in the next decade. They are beginning to read about their distressing symptoms, seek options for treatment, and look into the experiences of other women during this life-changing passage. Spirituality is a topic of great interest to many of these women. Even those who have been very pragmatic are faced with emerging thoughts of the deeper meaning of life and the prospect of death. These women are raising questions and seeking answers on a subject that they can no longer deny with cavalier existentialism.

Barbara Ehrenreich, in her article "Coming of Age," explores what feminist writers are saying about aging women and thoughts of death.

> This is not a phase that ends in marriage or a Nobel prize or promotion to branch manager (though all those things could well happen at any point). This is a phase that ends in death. Like it or not, the great spiritual task of the later years is not to be busier, prettier, or more productive than anyone else, but to be prepared for the fact of death. And this is one task, the philosophers agree, that cannot be accomplished in a condition of terminal busy-ness. ...
>
> The fact is that we will be dead when we die—and nothing in our individualistic, competitive souls prepares us to think not just of "death," in the sense of a deadline, but of actually being dead: as in *no more me*.[1]

Popular secular books are attempting to satisfy women's mid-life question for meaning with a mixture of medical data, non-medical methods of treatment, and spiritual panaceas. Those spiritual prescriptions include answers to questions about meaning and power in life and acceptance of death. But are they trustworthy?

Take a look at what many women are reading as they pursue spiritual questions.

Alternative Spiritual Remedies

Gayle Sand wrote a particularly funny book about menopause entitled *Is It Hot in Here or Is It Me?* Sand has been a columnist, restaurant critic, and editor-at-large for a Florida newspaper. Her book chronicles her search for relief from ravaging hot flashes. Determined not to use HRT, Sand turned to the New Age marketplace to find a cure. Her escapades took her from acupuncture to a drink from the famed Fountain of Youth in Florida. Some of the other approaches she tried had distinctly spiritual components. One example was a visit to a spiritual healer.

> My hairdresser, Sylvie, a very spiritual vegetarian, suggested that I visit Hilda, a spiritual healer. According to Sylvie, Hilda was the real thing: "She was struck by lightning when she was three, was meditating at four, and was healing pets at five. Then they wrote her up in the *National Enquirer.*" The *Enquirer* is not exactly *The New England Journal of Medicine* but I was still impressed. I think you should get a second opinion, even with faith healers, so I asked around. I spoke to several of the healer's satisfied healees and they all said the same thing: "Let Hilda lay hands on your menopause."[2]

Hilda didn't heal Sand. None of her New Age attempts helped. She ended up taking hormones after all.

Sand presented her spiritual adventures with humor, but admitted she had been willing to try anything to find relief from her debilitating hot flashes. Had any of the New Age remedies provided the relief she sought, she probably would have practiced them willingly.

Gail Sheehy writes about spirituality in mid-life in a more serious tone. Her book, *Silent Passage*, includes a chapter entitled "Wisewoman Power" that explains her spiritual views.

> Wisdom, or the collective practical knowledge of the culture that is more simply termed common sense, has continued up through history to be associated with older women. Even in premodern times, when Christianity rejected females as deities or primary healers, great public women did emerge and exert their influence through the religious system. Some became prized as advisers to emperors and popes, turned to for their healing powers, venerated as holy—and it turns out that they were usually near fifty when they took on this aura of wisewoman.[3]

How to Respond

We have a choice in how we respond to the teaching in these and other popular books on menopause. We can judge and condemn women who delve into books offering non-Christian spirituality, or we can engage with them so that we have an opportunity to understand these women and impact their thinking.

We can judge and condemn women who delve into books offering non-Christian spirituality, or we can engage with them so that we have an opportunity to understand these women and impact their thinking.

We can go through this time of life focused on ourselves (admittedly, that is often all we can handle). Or we can look around us and see millions of other women in the same boat in need of true answers.

Menopausal symptoms can last for up to ten years. Most of us don't experience a nonstop need to focus on ourselves during all those years. In those moments or months of calm, we can venture out into the lives of other women and seize the opportunity for impact. If we have no idea what women outside the Christian community are reading and thinking, it is unlikely we will generate much curiosity about how a relationship with Jesus Christ changes lives and overcomes death.

As Christians, we are not to dabble in spurious, spiritual teachings of the world. I am not suggesting that we become experts on the New Age and metaphysical doctrines suggested in so many of the secular books on the market today. But maybe we need to have a better understanding of what is out there. I do think we need to be aware of the tremendous interest in spirituality and seek to present the message of the Gospel.

In reading these books, I have noticed the authors' desires for spiritual truth. Even the most ardent feminists are opening the door for discussions about faith. Germaine Greer wrote a stinging book, *The Change*, which lashes out at the medical community and rallies her readers with a clarion call to denounce sexual stereotypes and grasp the power menopause produces. Near the end of this book, she actually acknowledges the potential place of traditional religion in the life of menopausal women. She writes:

> Religion is one of the easiest ways that the aging woman can unlock the door to her interior self. If she has been an unreflective Christian or Hindu or Muslim or Jew or Buddhist she may find it easier to find her interior life by entering more deeply into the implications of her religion. Examples of the piety of older women are to be seen on all sides; what is not so easy to discern is the joy that entering into the intellectual edifices of the great religions can give to those who have faith.[4]

Greer's view, like that of many secular women, is that Christianity produces little joy. Since religion holds little appeal to the unchurched, many of these women choose spiritual paths that lead them away from God and into themselves. How sad.

We, as Christian women, have much to offer women who acknowledge their spiritual thirst. We are unlikely to impact the writers of these books or leaders in non-traditional spiritual movements. But we come into daily contact with women who are buying these books.

Instead of simply dismissing these books as evil, we need to be asking ourselves, *What is the appeal of this kind of teaching? How can we have a greater influence on women buying into these methods?*

We don't have to compromise any of our own beliefs to ask these questions. We are not looking at what the secular market is saying in order to accept its doctrines ourselves.

If we find ourselves intrigued with teaching that we are tempted to embrace ourselves, we can test the spirit of the teaching. Scripture tells us the measure of the true Spirit of God.

> Beloved, do not believe every spirit, but test the spirits, whether they are of God; because many false prophets have gone out into the world. By this you know the Spirit of God: Every spirit that confesses that Jesus Christ has come in the flesh is of God, and every spirit that does not confess that Jesus Christ has come in the flesh is not of God. And this is the spirit of the Antichrist, which you have heard was coming, and is now already in the world. You are of God, little children, and have overcome them, because He who is in you is greater than he who is in the world. They are of the world. Therefore they speak as of the world, and the world hears them. We are of God. He who knows God hears us; he who is not of God does not hear us. By this we know the spirit of truth and the spirit of error.   —I John 4:1-6

If we remain in communion with God and His people, we will recognize error. If we are drawn to falsehood, we need to disengage. Some women involved in non-Christian spiritual pursuits may be trying to bring us into their way of thinking. We have power to engage with them for the sake of the Gospel, but if we feel weak and vulnerable, we can pull back.

When our spiritual resources are replenished, we can lovingly move back out into dialogue with nonbelievers and seek opportunities to impact them toward interest in knowing Christ. While we may not have a spiritual commonality, we have a gender commonality. Again, I say: Menopause is no respecter of persons. It will happen when hormone levels change. If it is a time of spiritual questioning, as it certainly seems to be, then it provides a great opportunity for us to reflect our relationship with Christ to those women who do not know him.

Looking for Relief

For women experiencing distressing symptoms during menopause, first and foremost, they want relief. The Christian may look to God for immediate, physical answers. In the safety of focus groups, these women frankly discussed what happened next.

Many of them admitted that in the early stages of menopause they felt that their faith in Christ would get them through the discomfort without medical intervention. Some of them felt guilty when that was not the case.

One frustrated woman who has emotional ups and downs said, "I should be able to overcome this. What is wrong with me? I find myself unhappy and living with uncertainty. I go to the Lord and teach Bible studies and listen to tapes, but sometimes I feel bad anyway. I get these waves of anxiety. I can be perfectly fine and a wave of fear comes."

Another woman gave an impassioned account of how she had gone from doctor to doctor to find relief for emotional stress. She had suffered from it all her life, but it worsened during menopause. None of the doctors took her seriously. Some of her Christian friends insisted she just needed to pray more and stop looking for medical help.

> *"In this world you will have trouble. But take heart! I have overcome the world."*
> *—John 16:33b NIV*

She ignored her friends' admonitions and finally saw a psychiatrist who diagnosed clinical depression. Her family had a history of depression and suicide. The doctor put her on antidepressant medication, which she still takes. She is a committed Christian who understands that her body needs medical help in order for her to function well. She has stopped feeling guilty that her faith alone couldn't make her feel better.

While there are certainly accounts of miraculous healings, many Christians appropriately make use of medical assistance to cope with varying forms of illness. Contrary to the idea that using medicine is a cop-out, one group concluded that God gave doctors certain gifts to use in healing. One of the writers of Scripture, Luke, was a physician. They saw no contradiction of Scripture in using medical means of improving life.

Other women found great relief in their relationship with the Lord. Their experience was just the opposite of the women who didn't find relief in spiritual pursuits.

"God's Word is life and health to my flesh," Amy said. "[Menopause] has brought me closer to the Lord. Other things that help me cope are Christian music, reading the Bible, praying, and fellowship. These things I really depend on."

As Amy talked on, she explained that the relief was not physical, but spiritual—an inner sense of well-being despite what she was feeling. She still has hot flashes and emotional distress.

"[My spiritual peace] coexists with the fragmentation."

Some other women felt that their spirituality was the only thing that helped them cope with menopause. When they felt overwhelmed with emotions, they would go off alone and pray. They would spend quiet time with the Lord and regain composure and experience relief. Whether they felt better or not, most of the Christian women in the focus groups agreed that spiritual comfort was crucial when dealing with the changing circumstances of mid-life.

The storms of mid-life come and go, but the peace that passes understanding remains. Women in a personal relationship with Christ talked about the presence of hope in their lives.

Peter expressed the reality of that hope in 1 Peter 1:3-8:

> Blessed be the God and Father of our Lord
> Jesus Christ, who according to His abundant
> mercy has begotten us again to a living hope
> through the resurrection of Jesus Christ from
> the dead, to an inheritance incorruptible and
> undefiled and that does not fade away,

reserved in heaven for you, who are kept by the power of God through faith for salvation ready to be revealed in the last time. In this you greatly rejoice, though now for a little while, if need be, you have been grieved by various trials, that the genuineness of your faith, being much more precious than gold that perishes, though it is tested by fire, may be found to praise, honor, and glory at the revelation of Jesus Christ, whom having not seen you love.

Peace and Pain Coexist

When my first husband was killed, the inexpressible comfort of God seeped into all the hurting nooks and crannies of my life and lifted me above the circumstances. I remember trying to explain this spiritual reality to a friend who just couldn't understand. He thought that I meant I felt no pain as a result of God's presence in my life, even as he was watching me endure a great deal of pain.

I tried to tell him how pain and peace coexist. I felt tremendous loss and piercing pain at the same time that I rested confidently in the assurance that God would see us through that terrible time in our lives.

> *But if relief means a life of spiritual fulfillment that coexists with pain, we have the only authentic answer.*

If relief during mid-life circumstances means only the complete absence of pain, Christians don't have the answer. But if relief means a life of spiritual

This is my funniest story from menopause …

Date: _____

RECEIVE

fulfillment that coexists with pain, we have the only authentic answer.

If relief from physiological symptoms of menopause means that symptoms must disappear, we don't have that answer either. None of the women I interviewed had hot flashes stop immediately during their prayers for relief—though there may be other women who were so blessed. But the relief that women did find was in the ability to handle the distress and discomfort of their symptoms.

Looking for Empowerment

Many of the secular books on menopause put a strong emphasis on self-empowerment. Some of this emphasis is in response to women being treated badly for centuries—sometimes in the name of Christ or the church. For women who have felt degraded all their lives, the idea of having power over their own lives appeals to them.

In her book *Woman at the Edge of Two Worlds*, Lynn V. Andrews writes:

> In this book I work with four of my women apprentices in Los Angeles who are experiencing menopause in very diverse ways. Together we build new ways of empowering our lives and the lives of our families through new spiritual integration with our everyday world.[5]

Some of the suggestions in these secular books hold great appeal, especially to women who are weary from being told what to do, think, or feel.

Many women in the focus groups expressed frustration over years of being told what to do. Some grew up in homes where fathers were domineering. I grew up in a home dominated by an angry father. I learned that in order to survive I had to figure out what he wanted from me and try to meet those requirements. He wanted perfection, and he wanted me to think like he did. When he couldn't control my belief in Jesus Christ, he seriously undermined my ability to believe that I could think for myself.

In a similar pattern, other women in the focus groups sat under church leadership that discouraged all but their own views. Questioning was synonymous with heresy. Yet the questions these women had were not related to salvation so much as "Who am I as a woman before God?" They felt pigeonholed by men who grouped women in categories that do not allow for individual expression or inquisitive thinking. These women were neither feminists nor men-haters, and for the most part, they were not angry. They were simply tired of feeling like they had mental limitations that distanced them from God and kept them from becoming who He wanted them to be.

We talked in the groups about the struggle for Christian women to strike a balance between being proactive on their own behalves and releasing control of their lives to the Lord.

Many women today feel weakened by the demands and expectations of others. But Jesus said that *His* strength—not the strength of an oppressor—is to be made perfect in our weakness. His words were, "My grace is sufficient for you, for My strength is made perfect in weakness"

(2 Corinthians 12:9). When power is relinquished to Jesus, the result is gracious leading. When power is abused by others, the result is often ungodly control.

The Growth of Faith in Trial

The deep, personal faith in God that can emerge from the fires of mid-life frees women to realize and fully experience their acceptance by Jesus. This power of Jesus is exciting. It requires a new kind of relinquishment. It is not a relinquishment of self that annihilates individuality. It is a surrendering of self into the hands of a loving God who, in turn, encourages growth, welcomes questions, loves unconditionally, and expresses Himself through the surrendered.

The women in the focus groups expressed less fulfillment in spiritual rituals and more fulfillment in personal encounters with their Lord. They are still reading their Bibles, praying, and going to church. But the essence of their contentment lies in their total openness with God, which results in knowing they are personally loved and accepted. They bring their doubts and questions to Him about true meaning. Their value in His plan is reaffirmed in their faith. They do not feel reprimanded for asking. They have not abandoned the doctrine of repentance for sin—in fact, there is much deeper repentance. It is remorse over inadequately loving God and others instead of regret over having broken a long lists of rules. There is less guilt over missing a church service and more concern about showing Christ's love to the world.

Self-Empowerment Changed to Christ-Empowerment

There is power in lives that are committed to Christ and surrendered to Him. There is contentment that God is in control even when it does not feel that way. Empowerment rests with the God of creation—not with our limited ability to make life happen as we wish.

> *Itt is the very nature of sin to prevent man from meditating on spiritual things.*
> *—Mary Martha Sherwood*

The unbelieving world grasps for the reigns of life, but its hope and reach fall short. While the teaching of self-empowerment holds great appeal, sooner or later, women realize that they really are powerless over so many aspects of their lives. Their choices may enhance their lives temporarily, but ultimately they can't stop hot flashes, look twenty-five, or live forever.

And when they are finally faced with the question of death, they have nothing to compare with the reality of eternal life found in Christ.

A Word of Encouragement

Isn't it wonderful that our relationship with God isn't based on how we *feel*? We are totally accepted by Him no matter what shape we are in. Through His Son we have access to God anytime, anywhere, and in any state of distress or frustration.

Spiritual realities, while sometimes difficult to articulate, bring huge blessings of inner peace and hope, even in the midst of pain.

196

Hi—
I'm at the memorial stone of a dear, dear friend.
The doctor said that her cancer was probably
estrogen induced.
Wishing I weren't here, without her—
Lois

CHAPTER 13

Facing Mortality

The secular world has little to offer in answering the question of how to face death. Some people believe in reincarnation, some believe that death is simply the end of existing, and others have no formed opinions whatsoever.

I was talking recently with a woman who is an atheist. She said, "I really don't care if I die and worms crawl in and out of my body."

I felt sad for her. If she really does believe that, she anticipates a dismal end. Her focus, and the focus of many women, is on living this life to the fullest at the present moment. It seems though that this viewpoint is harder to maintain as women age. It is one thing to focus on the present when much time remains. It is another to focus on the present when you may be close to the end of your life.

> *Yesterday is not ours to recover, but tomorrow is ours to win or to lose.*
> —*Lyndon B. Johnson*

That is one of the reasons why many menopausal women begin to think about death. The changes in their bodies during menopause clearly indicate that their years are limited. They are in the second half of life—at best. The reality of death is the crucible in which the Christian doctrine of eternal life rises victorious above all other beliefs about what happens after death.

Death is still an enemy to be endured, but for the person who has a personal relationship with Jesus Christ, immortality in heaven waits on the other side of death.

Behold, a Pale Horse

The book of Revelation is the account of the apostle John's look into the future. In Revelation 6:8, John depicts death starkly, "So I looked, and behold, a pale horse. And the name of him who sat on it was Death, and Hades followed with him."

I have heard the hoofbeats of the pale horse many times. When I was ten years old, my grandmother lived with us. I loved her deeply. But one morning I was awakened before dawn by the arrival of the doctor and

198

my cousin, Ron. I learned that my grandmother was dying from a cerebral hemorrhage, which had happened in the middle of the night. As she lingered on in her bedroom, I watched other people arrive: the minister, my uncle, and a few neighbors. No one spoke directly to me. They were busy, but I knew what was going on.

At 9 a.m., my mother asked Ron to take me with him to the hospital to pick up a rubber sheet. We rode in silence on our errand (designed, I knew, to get me out of the house). As we were driving home, I remember sensing the moment she was gone. The sky turned slate gray and a damp mist hung over the car as we crossed a bridge over the Brandywine River.

Nanny is gone, I said to myself.

I was cold. It was winter, but I was cold way down deep inside. Death is cold. When the pale horse comes, he breathes the frigid breath of the grave on those who watch him snatch life from the one they love. He rides off into the darkness leaving the pain of loneliness in the hearts of the living.

During the war in Vietnam, I heard the hoofbeats with frightening frequency. Calls in the middle of the night told my first husband and me that our friends had been ripped from life on earth while fighting in a jungle far away. Several women I worked with lost husbands and loved ones. Military funerals became a part of life. Death was always close by. When he wasn't sweeping in to carry off someone we knew, the pale horse was stomping the frozen ground of my memory. The telephone was an enemy. Every ring held the potential for more grief.

I was a Christian when most of these young men left my life. But I was not around other Christians so I viewed death as the end. In my late twenties, my first husband, Jack, and I became active in an evangelical church that stressed the doctrine of eternal life. I changed from seeing death as only the end of life to seeing death as an end that led to a better beginning. Jack and I were gratefully enveloped in this reality of eternal life for about six years before the pale horse rode back in.

When Jack was killed, I heard the familiar hoofbeats again, but the deep, cold dread of the past was gone. Death was still an enemy. Death still meant loneliness of heart. Death ripped my world apart in one dramatic swoosh, pushing a hot-air balloon into electrical wires and bringing it down in flames.

But this time, the rider on the pale horse was not the final victor.

> "O Death, where is your sting?
> O Hades, where is your victory?"
> —1 Corinthians 15:55

I knew that the moment Jack took his last breath he was in heaven. The loss was ours, the victory his. He was in a place of perfect peace. We would be together again. The Cross had overcome the grave and the rider on the pale horse could only touch us this side of heaven.

While the reality of heaven doesn't take away the pain of loss, it does give indescribable hope. Life doesn't end. Not only does it last eternally, it becomes a place of perfection instead of a place filled with pain.

Amazing Grace

Women in their mid-life years think about death. Many of us have been personally touched by the loss of a loved one. Many of us have already faced the invasiveness of disease. We have watched our friends receive news of illness and then endure treatment that devastates their quality of life. Despite the painful realities of aging, we as Christians have a hope that transcends our years of difficulty on earth.

One person who transcended such pain was my friend, Ann Reed.

When I came to interview her, she was sitting on a swing in her front yard, smiling. She looked beautiful— for any age. Her big brown eyes twinkled as she came across the lawn to hug me. I was amazed that this woman of beauty and grace was suffering the ravages of cancer.

Ann was sixty-seven years old at that time. When she was forty-two she had a hysterectomy. After the surgery, she was put on estrogen immediately. Ann did not remember being given any option. Her doctor simply told her she would be on estrogen the rest of her life.

Ten years later she developed a malignant lump in her breast. After this surgery, she was taken off estrogen. She remembered the menopause symptoms raging full force. She begged for estrogen.

"I said I would risk cancer again if I could only have estrogen. That's when my doctor told me my cancer was probably estrogen induced."

Her doctor told her that the surgery had removed all the cancer, allowing for an immediate breast implant. She had no chemotherapy or radiation, but the doctor refused to give her estrogen again.

Ann had no sign of any more trouble until October 1991. She was hurrying to answer the phone when she heard a bizarre sloshing sound inside her body. She went to the doctor thinking she had pneumonia. Indeed her lung *was* retaining fluid, but when the doctors drained it, they found cancer cells. Further testing showed that the cancer had spread from her lung to her liver. She began chemotherapy in January 1992. The treatment lasted for seven months. Then Ann was in remission.

The remission lasted about a year. When I interviewed Ann in August of 1993 she had just resumed chemotherapy. She was due to go back to the doctor to see if the therapy was working.

I asked Ann if any of her doctors had suggested a nutritional approach as treatment for her cancer, and she said they had not. Her doctors had agreed that there was no statistical proof that a nutritional approach would help.

Ann reaffirmed that her ultimate confidence is in the Lord.

"I was never angry. I never questioned, Why me? Why now? It is almost a settled condition that He is very aware, and my confidence is in the fact that He is the Great Physician," she said with a peaceful expression.

I couldn't keep the tears back as she spoke.

"The reason I am so earthbound is because it's all we know. Heaven will be so wonderful, but we don't know it experientially."

She told me that she and her husband, Kenny, talked openly about the likelihood of her death. She said that they knew they would be together again and this hope kept them from being morbid about it.

My prayer for Ann was that she would recover miraculously. But that was not to be. Ann slipped from earth to heaven on October 31, 1994. She lived and died with amazing grace.

Her example is what life is about: the amazing grace of God. He pours it out in the lives of those who invite Him in, whether for the horror of cancer or the ongoing stresses of menopause. As Christians, the promise of a pain-free future in heaven gives us hope now as we deal with the pain of the moment. In the book of Revelation, the apostle John gives us an image of that place:

> *In the time of trouble avert not thy face from hope, for the soft marrow abideth in the hard bone.*
> *—Hafiz*

> Now I saw a new heaven and a new earth, for the first heaven and the first earth had passed away. Also there was no more sea. Then I, John, saw the holy city, New Jerusalem, coming down out of heaven from God, prepared as a bride adorned for her husband. And I heard a loud voice from heaven saying, "Behold, the tabernacle of God is with men, and He will dwell with them, and they shall be His people. God Himself will be with them and be their God. And God will wipe away every tear from their eyes; there shall be no more death, nor sorrow, nor

crying. There shall be no more pain, for the
former things have passed away."
—Revelation 21:1-4

New Beginnings

We all want to experience wholeness. We want to be
fulfilled in mind, body, and spirit. We want to be
physically, emotionally, and spiritually healthy.

It is the spiritual component of our lives that pulls all
the other elements of healthy living together. Even in
poor physical health we can experience fullness of life
because we are encouraged by knowing that the troubles
of this world are temporary.

Keeping that in the forefront of our minds is not easy,
however. Bouts with physical and emotional pain are
not insignificant interruptions to our lives. They can
devastate us, thwarting our attempts to rise above
our circumstances.

Menopause can be a trying time. It is a time of change
and decision, and wholeness may seem elusive. Spiritual
resources may seem far away in the face of debilitating
symptoms and confusing choices. Even the most stalwart
of religious women may find themselves perplexed at their
inability to cope with life as they used to.

One woman, who has been in Christian leadership for
many years, was experiencing hot flashes and emotional
stress. Her doctor wasn't answering her questions to her
satisfaction, so she went to see a doctor that was recommended to her for his expertise in hormone therapy.
When he spoke to her in a condescending manner, she
cried all the way home in exasperation.

This woman is spiritually mature and highly adept at appropriating the means of grace in her life. Her faith has remained unshaken, but her usual calm in the midst of difficulty has been challenged since menopause arrived.

This time of life is a process. It is not a permanent destination. Time will pass, moments of calmness will increase, and the feelings of fragmentation will disappear. In the meantime, it is the spiritual component that keeps us as women moving forward. God is alive and operative on our behalf.

> *This time of life is a process. It is not a permanent destination.*

A Word of Encouragement

There is so much of life and opportunity still ahead. Wherever you are in the process of menopause, you can study and choose from numerous options for treatment. You can strike out on a new path that interests you or pick up an old dream and give it life. You can drink from the spiritual waters that God pours out on your life and let those personal blessings spill over into the lives of your family and friends. You can change and grow and enjoy life to the fullest.

Pain and challenges will not disappear, but you can meet them with wisdom and grace. You can move from menopause to maturity feeling good about yourself and your future. You can experience life filled with excitement and hope.

So much is ahead. There are so many new beginnings.

Writing now from the "other side" of menopause. The struggle through it wasn't easy, but I see how it has made me a softer, more compassionate woman. However, I _am_ glad I'm "over here" now. You'll get through it, too. Choose wisely, and trust in His strength—not your own.

Lois

CHAPTER 14

Women Take a Look Back

As I write this, I am in my mid-fifties and well past any troublesome symptoms from menopause. I still misplace car keys and can't remember names, but that condition is age-related and likely to continue. The ten pounds I gained during menopause still encircle my waist. My skin has dried and lost its elasticity. These signs of aging began during menopause, and they continue as the clock ticks.

If I were able to go back and change anything regarding my health practices, I would have started a weight-bearing exercise program much earlier. The silent onset of bone loss did its damage, and much of that could have been avoided.

On the other hand, I don't regret my decision to refuse HRT, especially since my symptoms weren't severe. I do, however, grieve the loss of friends who died from breast cancer, and I grieve for those who are now waging that battle. All of the women I have known who have had or currently have breast cancer took HRT prior to their cancer diagnosis.

I remember one morning during the greeting time in church when I moved in to hug a friend, and she stepped away from me.

"I'm sorry," she smiled, "but I am on chemotherapy and am trying not to catch any colds."

She extended a gloved hand, which I took and held in mine. She had been diagnosed with breast cancer some months before.

She went on to say that she had been on HRT and was taken off of it as soon as the breast cancer was discovered.

"But, you know, I wouldn't have wanted to die from heart disease, so I did what my doctor thought I should."

She died some time later from the spread of the cancer.

She died after taking a medication for a disease she didn't have and might never have contracted.

Today, many women I know are winning the battle against breast cancer. Early detection seems to be helping, and I am grateful for any progress made in the treatment of this frightening disease.

Date: _____

RECEIVE

This is my perspective on aging …

I am aware, too, that the deaths of several friends who were taking HRT contributed to my bias against taking it for myself.

The following stories will present varying views of women who are now past menopause and are looking back at decisions they made in younger years.

Elizabeth

I first spoke with Elizabeth several weeks before a doctor's appointment she had scheduled to reevaluate her decision to take Premarin.

"I started taking estrogen when I was about 47 years old," she began. Elizabeth, who is now in her mid-sixties, had a vaginal hysterectomy at age 33. It was not until age 47 when menopausal symptoms set in that she began taking hormones. Her hormone treatment has always been purely estrogen—not the common estrogen and progestin mix found in conventional HRT.

"I am so absolutely compliant when it comes to physicians, and I had an outstanding woman doctor who really felt this was the way for all female patients to go. I didn't dispute it in the slightest."

Elizabeth went on to say that her symptoms included memory loss, mild depression, and irritability. She also said that she had "tough times" during the first and middle of her estrogen-induced cycle.

"I was tired and weepy and just did not want to be like my mother. She was constantly awake with night sweats, was undoubtedly depressed, and was very dramatic and moody. All I had heard about menopause caused me to not want to be like that.

"Every friend I knew was on HRT, and [with my estrogen] my hot flashes did decrease. I still have these unusual circumstances of feeling bad the beginning and middle of the month. My mother had breast cancer, but the doctor still feels I should be on estrogen."

Elizabeth decided to be less compliant and much more direct with her doctor on a recent visit.

"I need to know from your lips," she said to the doctor, "what you think I need to do."

He told Elizabeth that the July 2002 test results from the Women Health Initiative showed no difference in benefit between women taking HRT and those taking the placebo. He also said that if she *were* taking the usual combination of estrogen and progestin, he would suggest that she discontinue; but he felt that since she takes estrogen only, she is okay.

Because Elizabeth feels better during the first and middle of the month while taking estrogen, she has decided to continue. She plans to return to her doctor every six months for reevaluations.

Judi

Judi started taking HRT when she was 44 to relieve menopausal symptoms.

"I felt like I was in somebody else's body. My emotions were so unlike me," Judi said.

She started with the lowest dose of HRT and moved to the second highest dosage a year later. During her sixth year of treatment, she was diagnosed with breast cancer.

"Initially it was found on a mammogram. [Since it was] high on the chest wall, it didn't show up well." Judi explained that her doctor said it was a cyst; nearly 18 months later, she requested a biopsy. Doctors were willing to do it, but they didn't think the investigation was necessary. When the mass was found to be malignant, she was taken off hormones.

"I had a mastectomy and am now on Tamoxifin. I also take low doses of Effexor, an anti-depressant, because it has been effective with hot flashes and with pain. I still have some pain from nerve damage from the mastectomy.

"My reaction to the recent study is confusion. [Medical opinions] seem to be changing with every study. I heard a doctor on *Good Morning America* say that they are finding in some parts of the population, HRT makes the symptoms worse; and [it] can actually do damage to the heart. [These] findings are the complete opposite of what they have said. …

"I was talking to my doctor last week, and she was saying that she is [constantly] frustrated as to what to tell her patients."

Mary

Mary was on estrogen for about eight years. "I had had a hysterectomy and my ovaries were removed, so I didn't take [estrogen] for symptoms, but because I thought it would be a good thing to do," Mary said.

After eight years of hormone treatment, she was diagnosed with breast cancer. Her doctor took her off estrogen immediately; she now takes Tamoxifen.

Mary went on to say, "You never know with medicine—things change. I don't feel angry because at the time [I chose to take estrogen], I wanted to trust my doctor. I'm not even sure he would say that [the estrogen] caused my breast cancer. I was on estrogen alone, not the combination.

"At the time I was diagnosed, it was hard because [I asked] the *Why?* question. I faced mortality.

"I was on stronger birth control pills way back when, and [I] wonder if that impacted [the onset of cancer]. …

"It's interesting how things turn around. Now that I'm on Tamoxifen, I have hot flashes. But I feel like I'm on the better end of it. A friend of mine breaks out in sweats on Fosamax [a medication used for loss of bone density]. Ten years from now, will they say Fosamax is bad?"

Nancy

"I went on HRT when I was 44 for menopausal symptoms. The symptoms went away. I would really rather live a pleasant life than to not be on estrogen and live longer."

Nancy is 65 now and was diagnosed with breast cancer a year ago.

"I had two areas [of cancer] in one breast and another area in the other breast that had a 30-percent chance [of developing into breast cancer], so I had a double mastectomy."

One month after Nancy's surgery, she met with her oncologist who saw no reason why she couldn't go back on estrogen.

"I wanted to go back on it because of all of the old symptoms. I am now on both estrogen and progestin, because without both I have no sex drive."

A Word of Encouragement

Everyone is different. Some women who have been treated for breast cancer are comfortable returning to HRT. Others won't touch it again.

The women in this chapter have faced decisions about treatment and have come to varying conclusions.

Fortunately, you have more resources and information available to you than they had years ago. You can be proactive about your health and make decisions that *you* feel good about. While your choices may not make sense to others, you know that God is still active and informs you in ways that sometimes neither you, nor I, nor anyone can explain.

Look not mournfully into the past, it comes not back again. Wisely improve the present, it is thine. Go forth to meet the shadowy future without fear and with a [brave] heart.
—Henry Wadsworth Longfellow

He will be with you and help you live a fulfilling life regardless of the type of health issues you face.

APPENDIX A

Starting a Support Group

The women in my focus groups truly enjoyed meeting with other women and talking about the specific topic of menopause. They appreciated hearing other women express feelings like their own with vulnerability and sincerity.

Some of these women have gone on to join or start support groups. They are finding encouragement and help in making their own decisions about menopause and other mid-life issues. Most of all, they feel uplifted and hopeful. The groups are a safe place where they can identify with their peers and openly share all of their feelings.

If you are interested in joining a group, try these: Check the calendar in your local newspaper that lists group meetings open to the public. Or call local hospitals to see if menopause support groups are available.

Or, you could start your own group.

Suggestions for Getting Started

- Make a list of your friends between the ages of 40 and 57.

- Call those you feel would be interested in getting together to talk about forming a menopause support group.

- Schedule your first meeting with the purpose of discussing what the members of the group most want from a support group.

- Host the meeting in a private home and in a room where women can talk freely without the hostess's family members overhearing the conversation.

- Agree to maintain confidentiality in the group.

- Agree to accept the validity of various forms of treatment, so that women can be honest about what methods they are trying or thinking about trying.

- Schedule your next few meeting times.

One Example of a Support Group

When I was going through menopause, I joined a support group started by a friend of mine. This friend, Carol, was interested in hearing what other women were experiencing.

We met in Carol's home on a Tuesday. The women who worked had flexible schedules, which enabled us to meet in the morning. We spent most of the time expressing where we were at that moment in our lives and in our menopause journey. It was a relaxed time of getting to know each other in the context of being about the same age and experiencing similar symptoms.

We decided to meet once a month. Our purpose was to share newfound information and update each other on how we felt and what choices we were making. Our group wanted to be able to talk freely and enjoy identification with other women who understood this time of life.

APPENDIX B

Using Postcards from Menopause

If you have daughters (or younger girlfriends), please take advantage of the Postcards from Menopause in this book. This supplement has been designed to be an easy, helpful, and personal way for you to share your experiences with your daughters or friends when they enter this phase of their own lives. Since they are likely chasing toddlers or working full time, the topic may seem irrelevant just now. But in twenty years, it will become a matter of pressing concern. They will be grateful for your forethought in preparing them for menopause.

Here in your own words, they can find answers to: *What were Mom's symptoms? What treatment did Mom choose? How were her relationships affected?*

As you write, keep in mind that your daughters will be especially interested in *your* experiences, as you probably share personality traits, coping mechanisms, and (in all cases but adoption) you share half of your genetic code.

There are sixteen Postcards from Menopause included. For extra sets for second or third daughters, call FamilyLife at 1-800-FL-TODAY (1-800-358-6329) or order online from www.familylife.com.

To use Postcards from Menopause:

1. Simply fold the cards along the perforation, and then gently tear out each card.

2. Read each and all card topics before you begin writing, since some of your answers may apply to multiple cards.

3. Write your responses. (If you're having a "jumbled" moment, use a scratch piece of paper to compose your thoughts.)

Remember, you're writing about *your* experiences and *your* decisions. While you're "always a mother"—do tread lightly. She'll be twenty years wiser, and twenty years more independent when she needs these.

NOTES

Chapter 1: What Is Happening to Me?

1. Wulf H. Utian, M.D. and Ruth S. Jacobowitz, *Managing Your Menopause* (New York: A Fireside Book, 1992), pp. 58-59.

2. Lois W. Banner, *In Full Flower* (New York: Vintage Books, 1992), p. 273.

3. Ibid., p. 285.

4. Ibid., p. 274.

5. Ibid., p. 274.

6. Mary Duenwald, "Hormone Therapy: One Size, Clearly, No Longer Fits All," *The New York Times,* 16 July 2002, D, pp. 5-6.

Chapter 2: Hot and Cold and All Shook Up

1. Dr. Sharon Sneed and Dr. David Sneed, *Prime Time* (Dallas: Word Publishing, 1989), p. 15.

2. Utian, p. 35.

3. Linda Ojeda, *Menopause Without Medicine* (Alameda, CA: Hunter House Inc., Publishers, 1992), p. 32.

4. Mary Beard, M.D. and Lindsay Curtis, M.D., *Menopause and the Years Ahead* (Tucson, AZ: Fisher Books, 1991), pp. 35-36.

5. David E. Larson, M.D., ed., *Mayo Clinic Family Health Book,* 2d ed., (New York: William and Morrow Company, 1996), pp. 441-442.

6. Winnifred B. Cutler and Celso-Ramón García, M.D., *Menopause: A Guide For Women and Those Who Love Them* (New York: W. W. Norton and Company, 1992), p. 150.

7. Joe S. McIlhaney, Jr., M.D. with Susan Nethery, *1250 Health-Care Questions Women Ask* (Colorado Springs: Focus on the Family Publishing, 1992), p. 544.

Chapter 3: Mind, Waist, and Emotions—What Next?

1. Utian, p. 58.

2. Ibid., p. 100.

3. Raymond G. Burnett, M.D., *Menopause: All Your Questions Answered* (Chicago: Contemporary Books, Inc., 1987), p. 19.

4. Beard and Curtis, p. 5.

Chapter 4: Startling Medical News

1. Gina Kolata with Melody Petersen, "Hormone Replacement Study: A Shock to the Medical System," *The New York Times*, 10 July 2002, A, p. 1.

2. Ibid.

3. Gina Kolata, "Hormone Therapy, Already Found to Have Risks, Is Now Said to Lack Benefits," *The New York Times,* 18 March 2003, A, p. 26.

4. Ibid.

5. Robert A. Wilson, M.D., *Feminine Forever* (New York: M. Evans and Company Inc., 1966), pp. 53-54.

6. Ibid., p. 116.

7. Ibid., p. 156.

8. Amanda Spake, "The Raging Hormone Debate," *Health,* January-February 1994, p. 47.

9. Hershel Jick, M.D., et al., "Replacement Estrogens and Endometrial Cancer," *The New England Journal of Medicine,* 1 February 1979, pp. 220-221.

10. Utian, p. 90.

11. Lisa Sanders, M.D., "Medicine's Progress, One Setback at a Time," *The New York Times Magazine,* 16 March 2003, p. 29.

Chapter 5: The Process for Making Informed Decisions

1. Patricia Anstett, "Menopause Treatment Challenged," *The Denver Post,* 9 July 2002, A, p. 11.

2. Kolata, 18 March 2003.

3. Chris Strong, PharmD., CPh., interview by author on 4 April 2003.

4. Lisa Dunham, M.D., interview by author on 20 March 2003.

5. Bill Radford, "Consider Risks, Benefits and Natural Options Before Dumping Your Hormone Therapy," *The Gazette,* Colorado Springs, Colo., 29 July 2002, Life, p. 1.

Chapter 6: Treatment Options

1. Strong, interview on 4 April 2003.
2. Kenny Harrison, PharmD., interview by Robyn Stutts and Amy Bradford, Little Rock, Ark., 21 May 2003.
3. Denise Grady, "A User's Guide for Those Who Choose Hormone Replacements," *The New York Times,* 23 June 2002, WH, p. 4.
4. Michelle P. Warren, M.D., phone interview by author in May 2003.
5. Chris Strong, PharmD., interview by author in May 2003.
6. Dunham, interview.
7. Bruce Kahn M.D., interview by author on 11 March 2003
8. Kolata, 18 March 2003.
9. Kahn, interview.
10. Isadore Rosenfeld, M.D., "My Advice on Estrogen," *Parade,* 13 October 2002, p. 8.
11. Ibid., p. 8.
12. Isadore Rosenfeld, M.D., "Second Opinion: Keep Bones Strong—Without Hormones," *Parade,* 13 October 2002, p. 20.
13. Ibid.
14. Harrison interview.

Chapter 7: Preventative Measures: Diet and Exercise

1. "Studies Vindicate Atkins' Diet: But Dieters Regain Much of the Weight," www.msnbc.com, 21 May 2003, http://www.msnbc.com/news/916555.asp.

2. Linda DuVal, "Lawsuit May Draw Attention to Dangers of Fast-Food Diet," *The Gazette,* Colorado Springs, Colo., 29 July 2002, Life, p. 2.
3. Utian, p. 118.

Chapter 8: Relaxation Breaks: By Yourself, with Others and with God

1. Richard J. Foster, *Celebration of Discipline: The Path to Spiritual Growth* (New York: Harper and Row, Publishers, 1978), p. 15.
2. Florence Littauer, *Dare to Dream* (Dallas: Word Publishing, 1991), p. 43.
3. Julia Cameron, *The Artist's Way* (New York: Tarcher/Perigee Books, 1992), p. 6.

Chapter 10: What Wives Wish Their Husbands Knew and a Mindset Metamorphosis for Every Grown-Up

1. Carol Henderson, "Divorce Over 55: The Bottom Line," *Woman's Day*, 1 February 1994, p. 23.

Chapter 12: Looking For Relief and Power

1. Barbara Ehrenreich, "Coming of Age," *Lear's,* September 1993, p. 45.
2. Gayle Sand, *Is It Hot In Here or Is It Me?* (New York: HarperCollins Publishers, 1993) p. 132.
3. Gail Sheehy, *Silent Passage* (New York: Random House, 1992), p. 144.
4. Germaine Greer, *The Change: Women, Aging, and the Menopause* (New York: Alfred A. Knopf, 1992), p. 379.
5. Lynn V. Andrews, *Woman at the Edge of Two Worlds: The Spiritual Journey Through Menopause* (New York: HarperCollins Publishers, 1993), p. 5.

Date: _____

Here are my words of wisdom for you …